"ACTIONABLE PLANS"

"Darryl always has the ability to clearly see the underlying causes and effects of actions and then develop actionable plans that take you to even greater success."
~ Quinton Martin, Coca-Cola North America

"HELPED ME OVERCOME MY FEARS"

"Darryl Mobley has an uncanny ability to boil down the most important considerations in living a fulfilled and happy life into simple, bite-sized, understandable, do-able steps. He helped me overcome fears of starting my own business. I now have two profitable companies, work from home to be with my kids, and call my own shots. Without the tools Darryl illustrated to me, I'd still be trying to juggle a 9-to-5 job, three kids, a husband, and a home, and no one would be happy."
~ Nancy Sur, DaCosta Global

"CREATED JOY AND LOVE!"

"Darryl Mobley has given me invaluable advice and insight regarding my business challenges as well as my personal crises. Darryl's own success across a wide spectrum of business interests is eclipsed only by the joy and love he has fostered in his own family. I depend on his balanced perspective regarding the things that should really take priority in my life. His assistance and counsel was specifically instrumental in getting me re-engaged in living my life to the fullest and attaining new heights in my career."
~ John DePiazza, Sacramento, CA

"THE BEST INVESTMENT YOU CAN MAKE"

"Over the years I have faced forks in the road, challenging situations, and troublesome bosses. Darryl's process allowed me to get clarity on the paths I should take in order to maximize the results I get in every area of my life. Darryl helps you to get clear on your goals and purpose – then you will develop your own incredible blueprint that will take you step-by-step to your life goals. If you want to live a great life, then the time spent with Darryl is the best investment you can make."
~ Dwain Celistan, Executive Vice President - DHR International

"DARRYL IS A WALKING INSPIRATION"

"I met Darryl Mobley years ago… Darryl stood out because he was not afraid to be himself through his work. His confidence and magnetic personality were highly motivating and inspired me to become an entrepreneur. I don't believe I would have thought that, 'I can do that,' if I hadn't seen Darryl… Darryl is a walking

inspiration. When he says, 'enjoy life,' people should listen. He knows how to do it."
~ Jim Chastain, Founder, RealityCheck

"THANKS FOR SAVING MY MARRIAGE!"

"Darryl is a wonderful gift to the world. It was so touching to hear the passion in his voice about how to create a better relationship. Darryl, I asked my spouse the question that you said would "dramatically and instantly improve" a relationship. It worked! It is amazing how powerful this question is. Before your seminar I was talking about divorcing my husband. I feel hopeful again for the first time in years. I want to thank you for helping me to get my marriage back on the right track."
~ Peggy [Last Name Withheld By Request], New Jersey

"I RECOMMEND DARRYL 100%!"

"Conversations with Darryl Mobley… will uncover exciting new possibilities for your family, relationship, finances, career, health and more. I recommend Darryl 100%!"
~ Les Brown, Legendary Motivator, Author and TV Show Host

"DARRYL'S COACHING WAS LIFE ALTERING!"

"His clarity of thought, focused questions, and insights into how people are motivated and how things really work was amazing and life altering for me! As a coach, he is the best and is just what I needed!"
~ Kelli Richardson Lawson, President & Chief Operating Officer - OppsPlace

"LIFE CHANGING GUIDANCE"

"Darryl's clarity of vision, straight talk and simple common sense has helped me over an over again cut through the clutter and come up with practical solutions to make me a stronger, more focused person, with a better understanding of how to achieve my goals. Not only does he provide life-changing guidance – he delivers it in a way that is memorable and often funny. He always leaves you thinking and encourages positive action. Darryl is simply unforgettable! His advice and guidance is priceless."
~ Aly Johnsen

"A LIFE CHANGING EVENT"

"The room was electric with possibility during Darryl's presentation. And I was not the only one to feel it. The time with Darryl was a life changing event."
~ Tonya Hinch, President and Founder, LifePlanning Unlimited, Inc.

DARRYL L. MOBLEY'S

RESCUE YOUR LIFE

30 DAYS BETWEEN YOU AND A BRAND NEW YOU!

It Takes Just Minutes Each Day to Live Your Best Life

Happiness, wealth, health, better relationships, a positive attitude, fulfillment, a stronger family life, and personal power are within your reach in just 30 days.

Now, Darryl L. Mobley, the Number 1 Life & Executive Coach, who serves clients on six of the seven continents, offers you the step-by-step information you need to live a happier and more successful life.

In this inspiring and empowering work, you will find a personal message and specific action-steps for each of thirty straight days. Why thirty days? Because Darryl knows from experience with his many clients that it can take you just one month to make the fantastic and lifelong changes that will take your life – personally and professionally – from stuck to superb. You will learn to uncover and activate all of your inner powers and resources, to attract the people and situations that honor you, and to create important relationships that are heaven on earth.

Let Darryl's strategies for daily success help you reap all the rewards that come when you begin living your best life. Start today. There really are just thirty days between you and a brand new you!

Praise For Darryl L. Mobley

"DARRYL HELPED ME THINK BIGGER AND BE MORE CREATIVE"

"I sensed almost immediately that Darryl was a strong ally and that he did not just seek greatness for himself, but that he wanted it for those around him as well. He listened more than he talked, but he clearly communicated his position on various business & life topics. His comments came in the form of questions, not statements, and he quickly allowed me to get to the right answer without ever 'telling' me what it was. The most compelling question Darryl ever shared was a simple greeting he wrote on a holiday card: 'How Great Will You Choose to Be?' I have thought more of that card from Darryl over the years than all the other cards I have received. There have been many significant influences in shaping my life, values, and careers, but there is absolutely no question that Darryl Mobley helped me think bigger, work harder, and be more creative in my career and helped shape the philosophies that we share with students at Making It Count."
~ Patrick S. O'Brien, Co-Founder, Making It Count

"DARRYL WILL MAKE YOU BETTER IN BUSINESS... BETTER IN LIFE!"

"We live in a world today of 'spin' and 'positioning.' Where the truth is often difficult to ascertain and good old-fashioned 'straight talk' is a thing of the past. Darryl Mobley is a breath of fresh air. A man of clarity, calling it as he sees it. Blunt, transparent, honest, courageous, with a great dose of common sense. Darryl had a major impact on our organization. His credibility was instantaneous and his perspective was valued by all — from work-life balance to career perspective, to time management... Darryl left his unique imprint of truisms and common-sense ideas on everyone. I can't count the number of people who came up to me to expound on personal learnings they gleaned from Darryl that will help make them better in the business, better in life — in short, better people."
~ Jim Lafferty, CEO – British American Tobacco Company

"MADE ME PASSIONATE ABOUT LIFE!"

"Darryl challenged me to think about not only what would be right, but what would make me passionate about my life. He pushed me to challenge conventional wisdom, discover the real issues facing me and then develop a compelling plan that would lead me to my goals. Never before had someone pushed me for my thinking, demanded I overcome my own timidity and reluctance, and offer my best. I have never forgotten those lessons and I use them everyday."
~ Anne French, Marketing Consultant

"I FEEL HAPPIER AND A SENSE OF URGENCY THAT I NEVER FELT BEFORE!"

"Since hearing your speech, I have made a conscious effort to identify certain goals regarding my aspirations as an engineering student and for the future of my personal life. Your speech motivated me to make significant changes including deciding and making plans to live in a new part of the country, applying to and scheduling interviews with several companies in that area, spending more time with my family, working out more regularly, and even pursuing possible love interests. I am amazed that the simple change in attitude you suggested can have such a powerful effect. I am truly grateful for the impact you have had on the way I approach each day."
~ Nicholas J. Gilligan, Senior, Mechanical Engineering, Worcester Polytechnic Institute

"DARRYL IS AWESOME AND INSPIRING!"

"You were awesome, a breath of fresh air, and very inspiring. The material you shared will help each person on my team reach their fullest potential."
~ Chris Heiert, Marketing Director – Procter & Gamble

"DARRYL PRACTICES WHAT HE PREACHES"

"I truly enjoyed sitting there in Darryl's trainings, listening to him talk about the facts of life. I admire him because he lives what he preaches. He is inspirational. I've attended A LOT of corporate trainings. He is the best!"
~ Sylves Thierry, Manila, Philippines

"EMPLOYEES WERE MOTIVATED AND ENLIGHTENED!"

"Darryl's ability to engage and maintain the attention of a diverse employee population separates him from others. If you are looking for a person that will motivate your workforce and energize their commitment to the organization, Darryl is that person."
~ Dianna M. Robles, PHR and Human Resources Manager – City of Austin, Texas

"DARRYL'S WISDOM…"

"Darryl Mobley is a very charismatic and enchanting executive coach. Sessions with him feel like casual conversations with a long-time friend. His wisdom flows smoothly and hits the spot right smack in the middle, every time."
~ Ramon Basa, MD

"I AM NOW READY FOR REAL LIFE!"

"Mr. Mobley. Where to begin? You have changed me with your presentation on personal leadership and your answers to the questions that I and my fellow

students asked you after your talk. I was unclear about the journey that waited for me after graduation. But, I can say that meeting you has changed me. I am now ready for real life!"
~ Karla Todser, College Student – University of Arizona

"DARRYL EMPOWERED ME"

"Darryl Mobley's refreshing and novel approach to Work/Life Balance empowered me and the rest of the managers in the audience to identify personal and professional life goals and to make choices in favor of what is truly important."
~ Paris Watts-Stanfield, VP, Chief Audit Executive, Alcoa

"DARRYL EMBODIES LEADERSHIP! INCREDIBLE COMMUNICATOR!"

"Darryl… You have the ability to explain things in a way everyone will understand without talking down to people, have exceptional listening skills as well as incredible motivating and communication skills, and embody leadership. You gave our group great insights into the value of a "personal brand" and how to create one, which will serve them very well not only in their professional lives, but in their personal lives as well. As much as anyone I have known, you embody the principles you espouse."
~ Richard C. Reizenstein, Ph. D., The University of Tennessee

"A ROLE MODEL"

"During a tough time in my life, after a serious injury, Mr. Mobley not only mentored me, but he made me realize and harness my strengths. Thank you to the man who inspired me to make myself better, stronger, and smarter."
~ Heather DiSilvio, Captain – U.S. Army, West Point Graduate

"DARRYL IS REAL AND AUTHENTIC!"

"Darryl, I have known you for 24 years. I have worked with you. I have seen you in social situations. I have seen you at play. I knew you when you were single. I have seen you with your wife and children. Since the first day we met, your message to everyone you know has always been, 'You Deserve A Good Life.' And now, you have dedicated your life to showing people how to get the good life. I wish people knew how real and authentic you are. You are doing what you were put here on earth to do."
~ Mike Cammon – Chief Marketing Officer, Vault Financial Group

"I HAVE NEVER FORGOTTEN YOU!"

"It is not likely that you remember me, but **years ago you made an impact on me that made all the difference**. Darryl, I remember when you spoke to me and other students… You made such an impression on me… Your impact on my life has been incredible. My interactions with you and your influence led me to summer internships, which allowed me to make the money that paid my way through college, and opened the door for my corporate career. You probably don't remember me. But I have never forgotten you."
~ Frantz E. Alphonse, Duke Univ. & Harvard Business School – Managing Partner – AP Capital Partners

"YOU GAVE ME THE GUTS TO DO WHAT I WANT TO DO!"

"You gave me the guts to simply do things… When so many people come to you telling of how you changed their life, how do you stay level-headed knowing that you helped somebody change that drastically? Thank you, Mr. Mobley!"
~ Kyle Diaz, College Sophomore

"YOU ARE THE BEST SPEAKER I HAVE EVER HEARD!"

"Mr. Mobley… You were incredible! Your discussion on personal power and leadership made us laugh and get serious about our lives – at the same time! As you spoke I kept thinking – 'Wow!' I feel that the one hour you spent with us was worth maybe more to my life after college than all the college courses I have taken. I am focused. I believe that I can achieve my career goals. And I have outlined a plan for creating the life I want to live. Thank you."
~ Ric Browsen – Student at the National Collegiate Leadership Conference

DARRYL L. MOBLEY'S

RESCUE YOUR LIFE

30 DAYS BETWEEN YOU AND A BRAND NEW YOU!

Published by How To Create A Life Worth Living Books

RESCUE YOUR LIFE: 30 DAYS BETWEEN YOU AND A BRAND NEW YOU!
© 2014 DARRYL L. MOBLEY. All rights reserved. Printed in the United States of America and throughout the world as needed. Without limiting the rights under copyright reserved above, no part of this book may be used or reproduced in any manner whatsoever without written permission except in the case of brief quotations embodied in critical articles or reviews. For permissions, address Mobley Unlimited, Attn: Rescue Your Life,™ 8924.Pinnacle Peak Rd, Ste G5-420, Scottsdale, Arizona 85255 USA.

First published in 2014. Updated in 2023.

Want Coach Mobley to be your Life Coach? Send an email with your request, name, and telephone number to:
Hello@CoachMobley.com

Visit our website
CoachMobley.com

Notice: The information in this book has been fully lived, carefully researched, and all efforts have been made to ensure potency & accuracy. Darryl L. Mobley assumes no responsibility for any amount of reader success achieved during or as a result of following this information. All information should be carefully studied, clearly communicated, and completely understood before taking any action based on the information or advice in this book. The author wishes the best to you and yours.

RESCUE YOUR LIFE: 30 DAYS BETWEEN YOU AND A BRAND NEW YOU!
ISBN 0-9753244-6-2

1. Success.
2. Personal Development.
3. Inspirational/Motivational.

"RESCUE YOUR LIFE" is a trademark of Darryl L. Mobley.

Contents

	PAGE
FOREWORD BY DENNIS KIMBRO, PH.D.	XIV
INTRODUCTION	XVI
WHAT'S IMPORTANT?	3
DAY 1 - ON COMPLAINING	7
DAY 2 - ON ACCEPTING RESPONSIBILITY	10
DAY 3 - ON MAKING DECISIONS	14
DAY 4 - ON THE FUTURE	17
DAY 5 - ON GETTING RID OF YOUR FRIENDS	20
DAY 6 - ON ACHIEVING GOALS	24
DAY 7 - ON THIS BEING YOUR LAST DAY ON EARTH	29
DAY 8 - ON SMALL STEPS FORWARD	32
DAY 9 - ON NEGATIVE THINKING	36
DAY 10 - ON HOW TO FAIL	40
DAY 11 - ON ATTITUDE	45
DAY 12 - ON SURVIVING PERSONAL DISASTER	47
DAY 13 - ON GETTING REMARRIED	51
DAY 14 - ON GETTING UNSTUCK	55
DAY 15 - ON THE BLESSINGS OF DISAPPOINTMENT	60
DAY 16 - ON LESSONS FROM OLYMPIC ATHLETES	64
DAY 17 - ON DOING TOO MUCH	70
DAY 18 - ON DOING THE IMPORTANT THINGS	75
DAY 19 - ON A BETTER FAMILY & RELATIONSHIP	82
DAY 20 - ON GUARANTEED SUCCESS	87
DAY 21 - ON GIVING LOVE TO YOUR KIDS	91
DAY 22 - ON LIVING INSTEAD OF SETTLING	97
DAY 23 - ON WORK-LIFE BALANCE	101
DAY 24 - ON SNAKES IN YOUR LIFE	106
DAY 25 - ON THE FIRST STEP TO SUCCESS	110
DAY 26 - ON BEING A HEDGEHOG OR A FOX	116
DAY 27 - ON GETTING YOUR FAMILY ON TRACK	121
DAY 28 - ON YOUR DON'T-DO LIST	128
DAY 29 - ON YOUR PLAN B	131
DAY 30 - THE STRUGGLE MAKES YOU GREAT	135
WRITE A LETTER	138
WHICH WAY ARE YOU HEADED?	140
AFTERWORD	143
ABOUT DARRYL	144
CONTACT DARRYL L. MOBLEY	147

This book is dedicated to my children, my wife, my mother, and my father who didn't get the time he needed to tell me everything.

Foreword

      Several weeks ago, as I prepared to catch another flight to another city from Atlanta's Hartsfield-Jackson airport, I received a phone call that placed me in a land that few people have traveled. Calling from Austin, Texas, was a dear friend, Darryl Mobley, requesting that I write the foreword to his new book, Rescue Your Life: 30 Days Between You and A Brand New You! Without hesitation, I told Darryl that I would be honored. And now you, the reader, can begin to honor yourself by fully implementing Darryl's rich wisdom and embarking on this thirty-day journey and all that it represents.

      Each year approximately fifty thousand manuscripts find their way to an editor's desk and are eventually published. I estimate that if you searched long enough you would find nearly fifteen thousand different titles in the store where you purchased this book. And yet, of all the books you could be reading, you are holding Rescue Your Life. Fate, luck, chance, coincidence? I don't believe so. Nothing is coincidental. I am convinced that many times over the course of our lives, the Creator challenges us to be more and to do more than what we thought possible.

      I know nothing of your particular circumstance, whether you are young or old, male or female, rich or poor. I do know that you are in search of a better life–increased wealth, health, and personal fulfillment. What this book is about to reveal has been known by only a fortunate few. Ironically, the keys contained within have evaded both the educated and the illiterate, not to mention the least, the last, and the lost. Contained within this thirty-day guide are powerful tools that you can use, not only to construct a new life, but also to improve the lives of others and turn your dreams into reality.

      In the pages that follow, you will learn how to develop the "life-changing habits" of men and women who have gone from rags to riches; from breakdown to breakthrough; and from the garage to greatness. You will learn how to organize your personal life in such a way that you will achieve all of your goals and objectives faster than you ever imagined. But I must warn you. You must read with an open heart and an open mind and be prepared to act. All the noble thoughts, well-intended plans, and keys to personal enrichment are of little value unless they are placed into action. To begin a journey such as this requires an act of faith. You need the faith to accept new thoughts, new ideas and concepts that will enable you to not only grow in every dimension, but to preserve your emotional well-being long into the future.

You are unique. No one suggested that you accept this challenge; by listening to the still voice within you took the first step. What you seek, seeks you. So now I challenge you to not only use this touchstone for the next thirty days, but the remainder of your life as well. How you and I react or fail to react determines the course of our future. Trust me. Your faith will be rewarded.

   Thank you, Darryl, for allowing me to perform the first task on my thirty-day journey.

Dennis Kimbro, Ph.D.
Author, **What Makes The Great Great**

Introduction

Hello Friend!

How To Use This Book

You were not born with the knowledge of how to live your best life. Neither was I. We must learn how to do it. It's not always easy, but it is worth it.

The key to getting to the brand new you and getting the most out of the book you hold in your hands is to have an open mind to the new approaches and key distinctions that I'll be sharing with you. Take lots of notes right in the pages of this book. Outline your ideas. Detail your breakthroughs.

Just as important — start by focusing only on day one's ideas during day one of your thirty-day journey. Put the lessons of that day into action all of that day. Then, do the same the next day for day two's lessons. Do this for each of 30 straight days.

Most important — commit to taking massive and sustained action with the tips and suggestions that you find **before your head hits the pillow each night**.

I guarantee that your life will be dramatically better — in all the ways that are important to you — once you make the lessons in this book habits in your life.

I am happy for you. Today begins your thirty-day journey towards the life you really want.

I wish the best for you. When you succeed, I have succeeded.

Let's get started.

Enjoy Life!

Darryl L. Mobley

DARRYL L. MOBLEY'S

RESCUE YOUR LIFE

30 DAYS BETWEEN YOU AND A BRAND NEW YOU!

Please complete this and the next page <u>before</u> you read this book.

Today's Date: _____

What's Important To You?

	How Important to You? *Scale of 0, 1, or 2	Notes/Thoughts?
Family		
Favorite TV Shows		
Friends		
Fun		
Health		
Higher Power		
Key Relationships		
Parenting		
Personal Growth		
Social Media		
Work/Career		

*Scale: 0 = Not important to me / 1 = Somewhat important to me / 2 = Very important to me

Today's Date: _____

Which Way Are You Headed?

	How Many Significant Actions Have You Taken In This Area In Past 2 Weeks? Scale of 0-1, 2-4, or 5+	Your Most Significant Action In This Area in Past 2 Weeks?
Family		
Favorite TV Shows		
Friends		
Fun		
Health		
Higher Power		
Key Relationships		
Parenting		
Personal Growth		
Social Media		
Work/Career		

Every Day Is An Opportunity For A New Beginning.

Today Is Your Day.

DAY 1

Is It Time To Stop the Whining?

Stop Complaining and Remove Whiners from Your Life

There is a direct connection between negativity and lack of success & happiness. This connection is based on these **two universal truths:**

1. We attract what we think about most consistently.
2. The energy you spend on negative thoughts, conversations, and activities blocks out the energy, mental focus, and time that could be devoted to positive things that you do want. **Nothing is made better with negativity!**

Another truth: virtually all complaining is about other people or other situations. This means that when you complain your focus is not on the real key to massive success and happiness.

That key is the change you need to make in order to create and live your best life.

To create your best life and attract positive people, situations, and things, you must embrace the changes you need to make and eliminate negativity & complaining from your life.

Enjoy Life!

Day 1 Action-Steps

What will you no longer complain about?

_____

_____

_____

What are the 3 Key Ideas that you have after reading this day's tips & strategies?

_____

_____

_____

What 2-3 Actions will you take as a result of your Key Ideas (above) and when will you take those actions?

_____

_____

_____

How will you benefit from taking those actions?

_____

_____

_____

DAY 2

Is It Your Fault?

Accept Complete Responsibility For Where You Are, Where You've Been, and Where You Will Go in Your Life

Accepting Responsibility is one of the great super-powers used by both comic book heroes and real people who are happy and successful in life. As with Batman, Superman, Wonder Woman, et al - - If something in your life is not to your liking: **You take responsibility** for it. If you tripped and stumbled (made mistakes or failed) in the past: **You take responsibility** for that result. If you have a big decision to make: **You take responsibility** for making the call.

Taking full responsibility for your life's results - past, present, and future - will fully empower you to take the actions and make the changes that will give you the life that you dream of. **Blaming others or anything else for where you are and what you have or don't have is for losers and the perennially unhappy.** Let's say that you are now 40 years of age. Even blaming yourself for a decision you made when you were 21 - as if your advanced age would stop you from making the same mistake now – is a trap that can lead to you creating a self-sabotaging barrier that blocks you from making the changes you need to make now.

Here is an example of the power of Accepting Responsibility: "I got subpar grades during high school because I did not make doing my class work a top priority. As a result, I was unable to gain acceptance into a top-tier college. I will not make that mistake again. I will study 3 hours each evening so that I excel in college and qualify to get into a top-tier graduate school." You may fill in your own examples.

Here is an example of Not Accepting Responsibility: "I got subpar grades during high school because the teachers were too tough, and I had to practice with my volleyball team four days each week. I was just too tired to study, especially after helping out friends who needed me to talk with them about their relationships. Besides, none of the students at the top of my class is having any fun in high school. Plus - those elite schools aren't worth the money. There is no difference between colleges. I haven't completed my college applications yet because..." You may fill in your own example.

Here are just some of the things that each of us must take 100% responsibility for if we want to live our best lives: weight loss, weight gain, our child's behavior, the job we have, relationships, health, finances, happiness, where we live, smoking, goal setting, drinking, getting or not getting promoted, level of education, and on and on...

When you own your outcomes, you will own the solution to virtually any challenge you face.

Take responsibility now and you start winning and being happier immediately.

Enjoy Life!

Day 2 Action-Steps

What specific aspects of your life will you begin taking responsibility for?

_____

_____

_____

What are the 3 Key Ideas that you have after reading this day's tips & strategies?

_____

_____

_____

What 2-3 Actions will you take as a result of your Key Ideas (above) and when will you take those actions?

_____

_____

_____

How will you benefit from taking those actions?

_____

_____

_____

DAY 3

Make a Decision

"I find myself simultaneously frightened and emboldened by the reality that God is waiting on me to decide what I want."
~ Darryl L. Mobley

Decide. Now.

1. Decide - right now - to clear your life and mind of clutter so that you have room for your greatness.

2. Decide - right now - what you must have during your journey through this treasure chest called life.

3. Decide - right now - to live your life in 100% pursuit of what you must have.

4. Decide - right now - to change yourself to match the life you want.

5. Decide - right now - to take massive action in every area of your life.

6. Decide - right now - to hang only with those who are in sync with your aspirations.

7. Decide - right now - that you won't quit, you won't back down, and you won't give in as you pursue your major goals – even when the going gets tough.

Decide. Now.

                Ralph Waldo Emerson said:
"Once you make a decision, the universe conspires to make it happen."

The universe is on your side… if you make a decision.

Enjoy Life!

Day 3 Action-Steps

What decisions will you make before your head hits the pillow tonight?

_____

_____

_____

What are the 3 Key Ideas that you have after reading this day's tips & strategies?

_____

_____

_____

What 2-3 Actions will you take as a result of your Key Ideas (above) and when will you take those actions?

_____

_____

_____

How will you benefit from taking those actions?

_____

_____

_____

DAY 4

I Need You To Focus on the Future

Focus on the future.

I have learned a few things during the decades I've spent studying success. One of the things I've learned is that unhappy and unsuccessful people focus on their past. Successful and happy people focus on the future. Oh sure, the past does have a role among those who are successful. For them, the past is used as a ladder to greater future achievement. On the other hand, unhappy people use the past as a weapon of self-defeating torture, regret, remorse, and hopelessness.

So...basically I encourage you to join with me in saying: **"Bupkis to the past."**

Let me ask you a question: **"Where are you going?"**

`Would you tell me, please, which way I ought to go from here?'
`That depends a good deal on where you want to get to,' said the Cat.
`I don't much care where--' said Alice.
`Then it doesn't matter which way you go,' said the Cat.
`--so long as I get somewhere,' Alice added as an explanation.

`Oh, you're sure to do that,'* said the Cat, *`if you only walk long enough.'

Alice to the Cheshire Cat (Alice's Adventures in Wonderland)

Where are you going? (By definition, this question is future focused.) Personally? Professionally? As a father or mother? Financially? As a friend? As an entrepreneur? Health-wise? In your key relationship? As a husband or wife?

If where you are going is not where you'd like to be going... Change direction now!

Focus on the future. Don't live the past.

Enjoy Life!

Day 4 Action-Steps

Where are you going in your life?

_____

_____

_____

What are the 3 Key Ideas that you have after reading this day's tips & strategies?

_____

_____

_____

What 2-3 Actions will you take as a result of your Key Ideas (above) and when will you take those actions?

_____

_____

_____

How will you benefit from taking those actions?

_____

_____

_____

DAY 5

It's Time To Thin The Herd.

Dump Some Friends!

I am fond of saying, **"Your net worth is equal to your network."** In fact, I have an entire 60-minute presentation-to-corporations with that quote from me as its title.

Two other sayings I've heard over the years...

"You can't soar like an eagle if you hang with turkeys."
"You are the average of the five people you spend the most time with."

With those sayings forming a bit of chilling news, I strongly encourage you to...

Dump the friends and acquaintances that are not adding value to your life and are not making you better by their presence.

Why dump your friends? Because <u>life is too difficult to try to make the journey without strong and able teammates</u>.

If all you hear from your current circle of friends is how bad the economy is, how one of them is living

paycheck to paycheck, how difficult it is to lose weight, how the 'man' will never let the friend get ahead, how bad this or that co-worker, boss, or professor is, how difficult it is to find a good man, or similar laments; you are going to unconsciously start to pick up similar beliefs. The results you get in your life will suffer. As with computers, so with your life, "stuff in equals stuff out."

However, if you surround yourself with friends who hold themselves to high standards of behavior... friends who are optimistic about this thing called life... friends who are always looking for a better way to accomplish their major goals... friends who support your attempts to move your thinking and living to higher levels... then you will pick up or continue to exhibit similar beliefs and patterns of behavior.

You = Your Friends. It's just that simple. And, it's just that frightening!

What should you do with those old friends of yours who are inconsistent with where you wish to take your life?

If your old or current friends motivate you, celebrate your successes, and support your efforts to change; there is no reason to cut them out completely. Just spend a lot less time with them.

However, any old or current friends that belittle your efforts to move forward, that are negative, that try to pull you back to old, self-destructive habits, that slow you down, that deny you your greatness... I suggest you get rid of them pronto! You will not rise while clinging to these anchors.

And puuulllease! Don't tell me that you have to keep your brother, sister, or cousin as a close friend because they're family. Family members can be just as cancerous to your happiness as non-family. Dump them! (Of course, don't tell them that they've been dumped. Keep the family reunions civil!)

These are hard words. But, someone has to say it. Now, you need to get about the business of identifying, reflecting, and attracting friends who have dreams and behaviors that stretch your thinking to a higher plane.

Enjoy Life!

Day 5 Action-Steps

Which friends will you spend more time with? Which friends will you spend less time with? Which friends will you dump?

_____

_____

_____

What are the 3 Key Ideas that you have after reading this day's tips & strategies?

_____

_____

_____

What 2-3 Actions will you take as a result of your Key Ideas (above) and when will you take those actions?

_____

_____

_____

How will you benefit from taking those actions?

_____

_____

_____

DAY 6

Life Is Not Worth Living Without Goals!

Got Goals? Get Goals!

We've all heard the saying: "you reap what you sow." Let's update that saying this way: "A specific Action leads to a specific Reaction." What this saying means is that if you want a particular outcome, you must commit the particular action or actions that will lead to the outcome you desire.

The success you are capable of won't happen unless you commit specific action, consistently. Super-Achievers understand and follow this simple guideline to Success. They consistently take specific action to get a specific reaction, or reach a particular goal. They know precisely what they want out of life.

Life's non-winners take little or no action in pursuit of a clearly defined and worthy goal.

If you believe in yourself, you will raise your self-concept and determine precisely what you want. You will achieve the Success you desire.

If, at present, you don't know what you want out of life and/or you are having trouble making progress in your life, I recommend you use my seven-step **Major Goal Master Plan** technique to get going in the right direction.

Major Goal Master Plan

Step 1 - Determine the Major Goal(s) you desire in your life. This Major Goal should represent the realization of your highest dreams. Be very specific in defining your Major Goal. Determine precisely what it is and exactly how much of it you want.

- **What is/are your Major Life Goal(s)?**

Step 2 - Develop an exact set of action steps (Strategies) that will take you to the Major Goal.

- **What are all the action steps you must take in order to achieve your Major Life Goal?**

Step 3 - Put a specific time frame around attaining your Major Goal.

- **Write down the dates by which you will take each of the Action Steps on your path to your Major Life Goal. Be sure and put down a date for each of the Action Steps.**

Step 4 - Since "Service to others is the price we pay for achieving our dreams," determine what service you will provide life or others in return for the attainment of your Major Goal.

- **What are you doing for others as you take the steps toward your Major Life Goal? Who - besides you - will benefit from your actions?**

Step 5 - Put your Major Goal and Strategies on the page you find (and print out) at...

MajorGoal.CoachMobley.com

After completing the Major Goal page, review your Major Goal and Strategies:
1) In the evening prior to sleep;
2) In the morning prior to beginning work; and
3) At midday.

Do this every day.

The Major Goal and your Action Steps represent your very own *Major Goal Master Plan*. Guard your Major Goal Master Plan as if it is your vault filled with jewels. (It's actually far more valuable!)

Step 6 - Take Action by executing your action steps every day!

- **Your consistent, daily progress will lead you to your goals.**

Step 7 - Share this Major Goal Master Plan only with your A-Team. Your A-Team should be made up of others who encourage you in your endeavors and make you better. Beware the "crabs in your barrel" that will belittle your self-development, diminish your enthusiasm and downplay your efforts.

This Master Plan technique will cause your life to take on a new glow! You will attract positive people and good fortune. You will develop greater inner-strength. Your increased achievement will amaze you.

Developing your Master Plan will require commitment to rigorous thinking and making choices. However, this is the route all Super-Achievers followed before they were Super-Achievers. Let me leave you with this...

> **"Are you in earnest? Seize this very minute!**
> **Boldness has genius, power, and magic in it. Only**
> **engage, and then the mind grows heated. Begin,**
> **and then the work will be completed."**
> *- Johann Wolfgang von Goethe*

Enjoy Life!

Day 6 Action-Steps

What are your 10 biggest life goals?

_____

_____

_____

What are the 3 Key Ideas that you have after reading this day's tips & strategies?

_____

_____

_____

What 2-3 Actions will you take as a result of your Key Ideas (above) and when will you take those actions?

_____

_____

_____

How will you benefit from taking those actions?

_____

_____

_____

DAY 7

You Won't Be Here For Long! It's True.

Today Is Your Last Day On Earth!

Today is the day that the universe has given you. **What are you doing with it?**

You and I cannot say what tomorrow will bring because it has not yet been given to us. But, we do have today. And that's why I say that **today is your last day on earth.**

Because today is your last day, you should feel as if you have nothing to lose, no truth to hide, no goal to avoid, no love you can't embrace, and no energy to save.

Because today is your last day, **I have some questions that you need to answer.** Here they are:

1. Do you want to continue doing what you've done today?
2. Have you engaged with your significant other the way you wanted to, today?
3. Did you eat what was best for you to eat, today?
4. Do you love what you do?
5. Do you love someone?
6. Are you doing something truly great, today?
7. Are you settling for less than your best, today?
8. Did you follow your heart, today?

9. Did you live your life, or someone else's life, today?
10. Did you listen to the voice of your inner giant, today?
11. Were you equal to your dreams, today?
12. Do your kids know that you really, really love them, today?
13. Have you hugged your significant other and your kids, today?
14. Did you write that love note to the one you love, today?
15. Have you laughed crazily, today?
16. Did you make changes to become better, today?
17. Have you been a positive influence on everyone you've encountered, today?
18. Did you take actions in pursuit of your major life goals, today?
19. Did you only love those people and things that love you back, today?
20. Through behavior and word, did you love yourself, today?

I don't know your answers to these questions. I would suggest that you look at the questions each morning and answer them each evening. I also encourage you to have a sense of urgency as you **follow your dreams and authentic loves**. Your dreams and authentic loves will never lie to you. They want you just as you want them. Everything else you do – other than following your dreams and authentic loves – is just background noise, at best.

You know that the clock-of-life is ticking for all of us. We have limited time to do our work here on earth. I ask you to wrap your arms around your special greatness and get busy.

If you knew that today was your last day, how would you change? Make those changes, today.

Enjoy Life!

Day 7 Action-Steps

What changes will you make in yourself—before your head hits the pillow tonight?

_____

_____

_____

What are the 3 Key Ideas that you have after reading this day's tips & strategies?

_____

_____

_____

What 2-3 Actions will you take as a result of your Key Ideas (above) and when will you take those actions?

_____

_____

_____

How will you benefit from taking those actions?

_____

_____

_____

DAY 8

Don't Be Bamboozled!

Have You Been Suckered or Do You Know The Truth?

In today's world, we are often seduced by what appears to be others achieving the huge score, the overnight success, and the big leap forward. When we trip, stumble, fall, or just don't experience immediate success in reaching our goals, we can sometimes become frustrated and even give up our pursuit. Here's the truth...

Success (despite what you see in the media) – in business, health, sports, fitness, parenting, weight loss, relationships... life – is almost always a matter of small steps forward. Immediate success is a dangerous fantasy.

My philosophy of success can best be summed up as, "One more inch." This view of life keeps me focused on taking the steps every day that will lead me to my goals. It will also work for you.

Think about it.

- Olympic gold medals are won - and lost - by inches.
- Football touchdowns are the result of getting an extra inch here and there.
- Surgeons deal in being precise at far less than a fraction of an inch.
- Weight-loss - while often sold as fast-happening snake oil - is a long-term race involving small, significant behavior changes.
- Getting - and staying - healthy is the result of doing small things right every day that - over time - lead to the desired endpoint.
- Raising children correctly means consistently coaching the small fundamentals into your kids (despite their best intentions to ignore you!) year after year after year.
- Politicians win with just one more vote out of a hundred than their opponent.
- Each of us learned to walk by trying to take small steps and then falling on our faces. We then got up to try it again and again.
- The stock market rewards focus on long, steady growth.
- Relationships - getting into them and getting out of them - is the culmination of lots of mostly little things done day after day after day.

Wish as we might, we cannot get to the top of any mountain in one or two big steps. It takes small progress over and over and over again in order to reach our goals. Once we accept this reality, we will be immune to the forces that seek to make us quit and give in when the going gets tough, goes long, brings tears to our eyes, and humbles us.

Put together your plan for achieving your goals. Be as detailed (step-by-step) as possible. Start with the first step and make progress each and every day.

I'll see you at the finish line!

Enjoy Life!

Day 8 Action-Steps

Outline your plan for achieving your goals… now!

_____

_____

_____

What are the 3 Key Ideas that you have after reading this day's tips & strategies?

_____

_____

_____

What 2-3 Actions will you take as a result of your Key Ideas (above) and when will you take those actions?

_____

_____

_____

How will you benefit from taking those actions?

_____

_____

_____

DAY 9

The Enemy Is Within.

Is Negative Thinking Destroying You?

Yes. It is.

The incredible beauty of the human mind - of your brain - is that **it can think about, imagine, or create what does not currently exist**. Your mind can imagine situations that are different from your reality. This ability to create new and better realities allows you to create a far better future than your present.

> "What you repeatedly think and say to yourself is what you get in life."

Your mind is like a computer, and the things you say to yourself act as commands that program your mind in the way you choose. **If you feed your mind with negative thoughts, you will experience a negative life. On the other hand, if you feed your mind with specific positive thoughts, you will experience a life consistent with your affirmative self-talk.**

What Do You Want From Life?

- Achieve your dreams and goals?
- Stronger self-esteem?

- More fulfilling relationships?
- More career success?
- Get rid of negative habits and attitudes?
- Better parenting skills?
- Exciting travel and vacations?
- A new home?
- Better health and fitness?
- Financial security and piece-of-mind?

"The conversations (thoughts, words and feelings) you have with yourself determine the kind of life and reality you experience."

The typical person repeats (in his/her mind) negative words - 24 hours a day, 365 days a year - regarding the situations and events in his/her life. As a result, these folks will attract negative people and situations into their lives.

Your self-talk will either build you up or tear you down. It is the way you use your internal conversation that determines whether you will manifest positive or negative results.

"Whether You Believe You Can Or Can't, You're Right."
~ Henry Ford

Most people aren't aware that they constantly repeat negative statements in their minds. **Do you tell yourself that you can't do something, that you are no good, unattractive, too short, too weak, too fat, too thin, too old, too young, too uneducated, or that you could never do this or that?** You must understand that your subconscious mind accepts as true whatever you repeat to it - your programming - and will eventually **attract situations and people who are consistent with your programming, whether it is good or bad for you**.

The Power of Affirmations

Affirmations are statements that describe in positive words a situation, event, habit, or goal - that you really want - and which you repeat to yourself aloud. When you repeat affirmations often and in a very specific way, they take root in your subconscious mind and influence it (you!) to act in a manner consistent with the affirmations.

Repeat your affirmations with passion, belief, and focus, and they will change the programming of your subconscious mind, which transforms the way you think, your habits, your actions, your attitudes, and the results you get. Simply put, affirmations will help you create your best life and attract better opportunities.

> "You must refuse to think negative thoughts,
> if you wish to get positive results."

Change your thinking.

Enjoy Life!

Day 9 Action-Steps

Write 10 affirmations below.

_____

_____

_____

What are the 3 Key Ideas that you have after reading this day's tips & strategies?

_____

_____

_____

What 2-3 Actions will you take as a result of your Key Ideas (above) and when will you take those actions?

_____

_____

_____

How will you benefit from taking those actions?

_____

_____

_____

DAY 10

I've Got 12 Commandments. (Not a measly 10!)

I Want You To Fail

Not really, but...

If I wanted you to fail,
like hitting your thumb instead of the nail,
I would draw up a list for you,
of just twelve things to do.

Here they are:

Coach Mobley's 12 Commandments of Failure

1. **Don't make plans** to achieve the success you desire. What are your plans for success?

2. **Don't set specific dates** for the accomplishment of key parts of your goals. What dates have you set for meeting certain progress points towards your goals?

3. **Plan and plan and plan… without ever taking effective action.** When do you plan to take massive action in pursuit of your goals?

4. **Don't have a powerful, all-consuming reason "why"** you wish to reach your goal. Why do you want to achieve the major goal you've set?

5. **Don't be congruent with your goals.** What sorts of people do the thing that you have set as your goal? Are you that person right now? What will you do to become that person so that you are worthy of the goal you seek?

6. **Suffer from scatteration.** What are your major goals? What are the key action steps you must take to achieve your major goals? Are you prepared to eliminate, as much as possible, all the things you currently do that don't lead you to your major goals?

7. **Don't embrace what success will mean for you.** Have you decided that you really want what attainment of your goal will give you?

8. **Fear failure.** Do you worry about what will happen if you don't achieve your goals? Do you fear criticism or rejection? What resources will you seek out to help you get out of your head and into your greatness?

9. **Fail to focus.** What will you do to make sure that your every available moment is spent focusing on taking steps toward your goal?

10. **Keep negative, goal-destroying people in your life.** Are you allowing dream-stealers (negative people) to have access to

you? Do you accept that no one has the right to drain you of your positive energy? Have you developed strategies for eliminating negative dream-stealers from your life?

11. **Don't do the work that the goal requires**. Are you lazy? Are you willing to do the work that all real success requires? Why? Or, why not?

12. **Wait for the "perfect situation" to present itself before you make your move.** Have you been making the circular arguments for waiting for the perfect situation? These arguments keep you in failure-pattern. This sort of thinking has kept people in… jobs they hate… abusive relationships… terrible cities… health damaging habits… declining stocks… and non-productive friendships. Are you willing to accept that there will never be a perfect time or perfect situation for you to make your move on life? Are you willing to make your move, now?

You know that I want you to succeed by not following my 12 Commandments. I gave a presentation to a major global corporation that was suffering – according to the CEO – from an inability to achieve key business goals and a focus on the world's bad economy.

The CEO told me that they had the financial, technical, strategic, and human resources necessary to achieve the organization's goals. What they were lacking was the attitude necessary for success.

I gave my presentation – consisting primarily of the 12 Commandments above – to about 17,000 employees. I then worked with the corporation's 11 key managers for four months on behavioral congruency. The result just eight months later: Each of the corporation's key business objectives was exceeded.

How about you? Can you <u>not</u> follow 12 simple commandments? This is one instance when I don't want you to follow my advice.

Enjoy Life!

Day 10 Action-Steps

Which of my 12 Commandments were you doing?

_____

_____

_____

What are the 3 Key Ideas that you have after reading this day's tips & strategies?

_____

_____

_____

What 2-3 Actions will you take as a result of your Key Ideas (above) and when will you take those actions?

_____

_____

_____

How will you benefit from taking those actions?

_____

_____

_____

DAY 11

The Attitude You Have Is The Life You Get

What Are You Getting?

Shape your attitude and design your destiny by going to the web page you find (and print out) at...

Success.CoachMobley.com

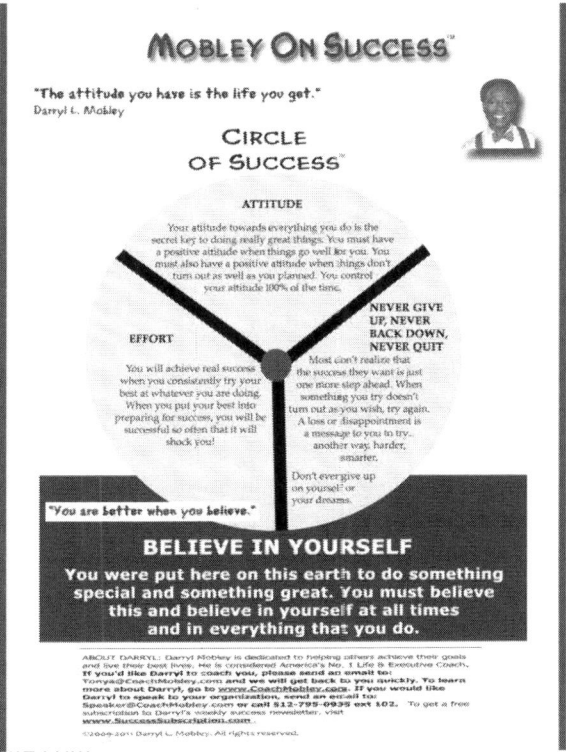

Day 11 Action-Steps

Describe your attitude.

_____

_____

_____

What are the 3 Key Ideas that you have after reading this day's tips & strategies?

_____

_____

_____

What 2-3 Actions will you take as a result of your Key Ideas (above) and when will you take those actions?

_____

_____

_____

How will you benefit from taking those actions?

_____

_____

_____

DAY 12

Are You In the Midst of Personal Disaster?

Tough Times Don't Last, Unless You Invite Them To Stay

If you live long enough you will be knocked to your knees by life. In fact, even as I write this to you, a series of fires has wreaked major damage to homes in my area of the world. None of us are immune to stuff happening. Given that simple truth, which of the following life-stressors are you going through now or have you gone through recently enough for the scars to be fresh?

1. You've been fired
2. You've lost your home to fire, or earthquake, or flood, or...
3. You've lost a loved one to death
4. You've gone through a divorce or breakup
5. You're planning a wedding
6. You're being ground down at work
7. You're raising kids
8. You're raising a kid who is seemingly always in trouble
9. You're in conflict with the in-laws
10. You're in debt
11. You're always stuck in traffic to and from work
12. You're studying for major tests

13. You're pregnant
14. You're having legal and/or tax problems
15. You're failing to reach a goal
16. You have personal safety concerns
17. You're newly married
18. You're experiencing personal illness or injury
19. You're having sexual difficulties
20. You're experiencing significant changes in the family
21. You're taking a new job
22. Your child is leaving home
23. You're starting college away from home
24. Your business is suffering

The more of these life-stressors that you've experienced, the more likely you are to suffer physical and emotional illness, unless you know how to cope.

Okay - I have your attention.

Here are my ten techniques for surviving and thriving (going beyond mere coping) during the chaos and stress of life:

1. Ask others for help. Going it alone will likely lead to heightened stress. (Hey! You can always send me an email.)
2. Be optimistic about the future. Nothing is made better with negativity!
3. Find role models who are dealing/have dealt well with life-stressors. Follow their lead. Copy winners and you win.
4. Help someone else get through the tough time. You will be amazed at the strength you have when you extend yourself to help others.
5. Stop watching, viewing, or listening to the news. That stuff will drive you crazy! (Obviously, you do need to stay aware of pertinent information that may directly and immediately affect you. But, most people go overboard with the amount of

negative information they willingly and unnecessarily seek out.)
6. Get back to your regular routine. Life goes on. So too must you go onward.
7. Feed your mind with positive information. (Shameless plug: Continue reading my books, newsletters, and emails.)
8. Seek to become a problem-solver (as opposed to wallowing in your problems).
9. Drink and smoke less than you do normally. Don't overeat.
10. Do things that are fun. What you do for fun will define your life. (How's that for a scary reality?)

To all who are feeling woozy from a current life-stressor, please remember that even in darkness there is light… if you believe!

What you do in response to life-stressors is a choice. I encourage you to choose victory, happiness, progress, success, and glory. They are all still possible as long as you are alive.

And, you are!

Enjoy Life!

Day 12 Action-Steps

Which of my techniques will you use today in order to cope with your tough times?

_____

_____

_____

What are the 3 Key Ideas that you have after reading this day's tips & strategies?

_____

_____

_____

What 2-3 Actions will you take as a result of your Key Ideas (above) and when will you take those actions?

_____

_____

_____

How will you benefit from taking those actions?

_____

_____

_____

DAY 13

Get Remarried. Please!

There Are Two Great Reasons You Should Remarry

A Confession from Darryl L. Mobley

As of the date I write this I have married nine times. Each marriage is better than the one before.

Let me stipulate that those of us who are in committed relationships must always be about the business of keeping the connection fresh and growing. Why? Unless we nurture our relationships as we would a treasured garden, the relationship ceases to be special.

A garden that is not regularly fertilized, weeded, trimmed, watered, and has insects removed, eventually is so far gone that it becomes an eyesore and in need of complete replacement. The same is true with your key relationship. A relationship that is not regularly cleansed of annoyances, protected from negative influences, and refocused on goals will eventually be so far gone that it will collapse under the weight of its own suffocating existence.

During a recent interview, I told the reporter that success in life, business, or relationships is a formula. If you work the right formula correctly and consistently, you will experience great success. If you work the wrong formula, you will fail. It's just that simple.

So - does your formula include the right elements to bring you relationship bliss?

But wait! Let me get back to my marriages. My first marriage was in a church several years ago. It was great. Lots of friends were in attendance. Minister. Week-long bachelor's party in a Winnebago that crisscrossed in and out of the United States. Cake in the face. The whole nine yards.

Since then, my marriages have occurred near a Dunkin Donuts in Vermont, on the campus of Princeton University, outside a Legal Sea Foods restaurant in Boston, on a quaint side street in Hanover, New Hampshire, at a huge rest stop in Rhode Island, under a very tall flag pole in New London, Connecticut, and beside the fortress-like buildings on the campus of West Point. These marriages occur without a minister, a bachelor's party, a bunch of friends, or the expense. They are very casual.

It's time for full disclosure: I have married the same woman each time. Each marriage fits with my relationship formula.

Each of the marriages – after the first one – have been a surprise to my wife. Without warning, I will ask her if she'll marry me. She has said "yes," each time. (Whew!) I then pull out my marriage vow, and a camera to record the "event," and read my vow to her. We've been walking along a sidewalk, or leaving a restaurant, or standing in line for a plane when I've popped the question. The "ceremony" tends to happen right then and there.

Here's the delightful twist: Each marriage vow is written by me and is different from the other vows. My wife knows that I write each vow myself. This writing of a different vow each time gives me incredible bonus points with her. It also gives me bonus points with my kids, who are often around to witness the marriages.

Most importantly, asking my wife to marry me when it is **totally unexpected**, hearing her say "yes," reading my vow to her, and having my kids as witnesses is a powerful **affirmation of our**

relationship, serving to **recharge** and **renew** the life we're building together.

Recharge and Renew. Those are two of the reasons that I remarry.

Why are recharging and renewing necessary? Recharging and renewing are necessary because maneuvering through this thing called "life" can sap the energy out of even the best relationships. If you don't take the initiative to infuse your relationship with freshness, you will probably find yourselves growing apart and becoming strangers who happen to live together.

My goal is to remarry my wife 1,000 times. What about you? What's your formula for relationship success?

Enjoy Life!

Day 13 Action-Steps

What impact will remarrying have on you, your loved one and your relationship?

_____

_____

_____

What are the 3 Key Ideas that you have after reading this day's tips & strategies?

_____

_____

_____

What 2-3 Actions will you take as a result of your Key Ideas (above) and when will you take those actions?

_____

_____

_____

How will you benefit from taking those actions?

_____

_____

_____

DAY 14

Are You Stuck?

Spinning Your Wheels? Not Getting Anywhere? Feeling Hopeless? Wondering If You Are Where You Should Be?

During a recent presentation that I made to an audience of female business owners I was asked, "What is the most prevalent problem that most people have?" I asked the audience member if she was asking about parenting, personal, professional... She said, "Overall." I told the audience that, "The number 1, most often dealt with problem that I see in people is that they are stuck. They are stuck in a non-winning and not self-serving way of thinking, believing, and/or behaving."

Perhaps you are stuck.

"Stuck" is where you are when you feel you don't know what to do next or now. Perhaps you are stuck in a bad or dissatisfying job. Maybe you are stuck in a less than fulfilling relationship. Or, you could be stuck and unable to start your book. You might be stuck hanging around underachievers or negative people day after day. Sometimes we get stuck in bad habits - overeating, smoking, excessive drinking, out of control anger, laziness, wasting time, lack of focus, spending time on worthless endeavors, procrastination, negative thinking, and on and on.

Enough of the gentle talk. The truth is that being stuck is a choice you've made. It is sad and true that many people become crazy-comfortable being stuck and don't really want to change! Some just don't know how. (That's where having a life coach really helps.) If you don't make the changes, you won't win.

In order to get out of stuck, **you need to change your beliefs, which will cause a change in your thinking, which will lead to a change in your behavior**. One of the ways I work with my "stuck" clients to get them to change their beliefs, thinking and behavior is through the use of questions. I ask them questions and demand answers. But I don't ask just any old questions. I am known to be very direct, even blunt.

Let me share some of the questions with you.

Questions Darryl Might Ask You, If You Were Brave Enough To Let Him

Here are some questions that can get you unstuck and moving quickly towards your highest possibility.

- How can I do it differently, smarter, and faster?
- How many ways can I get unstuck? (Develop a list. Now!)
- What would I do if I did know what to do?
- What do I want to accomplish before I leave this life?
- What kind of relationship would I like to have with my mate?
- What do I want to do in my life?
- What do I want to own that I don't own?
- How great do I want to be?
- What would I do if I didn't care what anyone thought?

- What would I do if I knew my parents would never find out?
- What would I do if I knew I could not fail?
- What would I do differently if I forgave myself for the mistakes I've made?
- Who else has done what I want to do, and am I studying them?

Now - here is the masterstroke: <u>Let your answers direct your actions</u> and you may never again be stuck.

Here's more on making progress in your life.

GET OUT OF PARK

My friend Les Brown – the great motivational speaker - told me about a time when he had a big personal failure, and he just pulled over (metaphorically speaking) and parked his life. He got stuck wallowing in the disappointment he had experienced. He finally asked himself the right questions and got unstuck. He and I joke that anytime you find yourself going through Hell - - make sure that you don't stop. Keep moving until you get out.

ASK FOR HELP

I have found that the best way for me to get better results is to ask others for input. But wait! The key to you asking for help is to ask the right people for input. Don't ask those who are also stuck. Don't ask perennial losers. (Yes. I know that's harsh. It's also true.) Don't ask advice of people who have not succeeded in the area you wish to succeed in.

UPLEVEL YOUR CIRCLE OF FRIENDS

You will remain stuck as long as your network is full of the happily stuck or those with negative attitudes. Get out of the crab barrel, now!

BANISH "YEAH, BUT" FROM YOUR LIFE

When we say "yes" we move toward our highest being. When we follow "yeah" with "but," we place a sticky goo on our shoes that stops us from moving toward our passion-filled best life. Saying "yeah, but" is a horrendous habit. I make it a habit to avoid "yeah, but" people like the plague.

You were put here on this earth to live your best life. You were put here to do something special --- to leave your unique mark. Get unstuck now!

Enjoy Life!

Day 14 Action-Steps

What will you do to get unstuck?

_____

_____

_____

What are the 3 Key Ideas that you have after reading this day's tips & strategies?

_____

_____

_____

What 2-3 Actions will you take as a result of your Key Ideas (above) and when will you take those actions?

_____

_____

_____

How will you benefit from taking those actions?

_____

_____

_____

DAY 15

Have You Ever Been Disappointed? Great!

The Blessings of Disappointment

Everyone is provided chances to deal with failures, disappointments, and defeat. You may be a teenager absorbing the impact of a less-successful-than-desired sports season, a business person dealing with sales that fall below your needs, a parent who has been unable to communicate with a troublesome child, a college student absorbing a bad grade on a major test, or a spouse coping with a relationship gone sour. How we come out of those stumbles is a reflection of our mindset.

I believe that we grow much more from what we learn from defeat than what we get from the glow of success. In fact, my long study of successful people, relationships, businesses, and winning teams shows me that the prequel to massive achievement is failure.

A short while back a very well-known coaching client of mine called me to discuss his professional team's disastrous performance in a big game. I suggested that he let his team embrace what I have termed the **"Blessings of Disappointment."**

Embracing the "Blessings of Disappointment" means that you look into your defeats, failures, and setbacks for the secret keys to the ultimate successes that you seek.

Here's how you can embrace the "Blessings of Disappointment," uncover those secrets, and live your best destiny:

Step 1 - When you fail to reach a goal you must evaluate what it was about your performance that was not up to the challenge. These are your areas needing improvement.

Step 2 – Resist the temptation to assign responsibility for the results you experienced to someone or something else. Why? When you give the responsibility for your situation or results to others, you give away your power. Being powerless is not where you want to be. Don't blame the weather, the economy, your team's lack of experience, your bonehead boss, or your mother-in-law. Accepting total responsibility is akin to a comic book hero's super power. I like to say "Losers Blame Others while Winners Claim Responsibility."

Step 3 – Develop specific action steps (for each of your areas-that need-improvement) that can change the outcome you experienced from defeat to success. These action steps are the secret keys to your ultimate success.

Step 4 – Take the action steps that you have developed, and that will lead to a different outcome for you. Don't stop. Don't back down. Don't accept the failure as the way it has to be. You will move closer to your ultimate success once you take action with the secret keys.

Thomas Alva Edison said, "I have not failed. I've just found 10,000 ways that won't work." Clearly, Mr. Edison used his "10,000 ways" that didn't work to uncover what did work and achieve his ultimate success.

Basketball's Michael Jordan said, "I've missed more than 9000 shots in my career. I've lost almost 300 games. 26 times, I've been trusted to take the game winning shot and missed. I've failed over and over and over again in my life. And that is why I succeed."

Everyone learns to speak by first uttering unintelligible gibberish. Each failure to properly form words brings the baby closer to brilliant orator.

The simple truth is that very little is learned from success. Achieving success is why it is so difficult for professional teams to repeat as champions. When we succeed, we tend to relax and think that we are good enough as we are.

Failure announces loudly that we were not equal to the challenge. If we are honest, we will take from failure that we need to make changes in order to win. That awareness is the blessing.

And so it is. **You cannot succeed without failure preceding.**

What you learn from your failures will be far more productive than what you get from victory. This is why I want you to embrace the "Blessings of Disappointment."

Enjoy Life!

Day 15 Action-Steps

What has disappointed you?

_____

_____

_____

What are the 3 Key Ideas that you have after reading this day's tips & strategies?

_____

_____

_____

What 2-3 Actions will you take as a result of your Key Ideas (above) and when will you take those actions?

_____

_____

_____

How will you benefit from taking those actions?

_____

_____

_____

DAY 16

6 Life and Business Success Lessons I Learned From Olympic Athletes

What Olympians Know (And So Should You!)

May I share a secret with you?

Many years ago, when I was seriously into my athletic goals, **I had the great fortune to train around and with, and to observe training, some of history's greatest Olympians.** Big-timers like *Edwin Moses, Mary Decker Slaney, Eric Heiden, Evelyn Ashford, Henry Marsh, Flo Hyman, Al Oerter*, as well as a hall-of-fame list of other divers, track stars, gymnasts, swimmers, hockey players, volleyball players, team handball players, wrestlers, and so

on. (I also met **the legendary Jesse Owens** - who gave me an inspiring pep talk and shared a life lesson – while I was rehabbing my jacked-up shoulder and elbow at the Olympic Training Center in Colorado Springs, Colorado. But, that's a topic for another book.)

That's me (on the right) in the photo on the previous page back in the day with the great Al Oerter - the only athlete to win the same Olympic event four times in a row, setting Olympic records each time. That's right. Al was a four-time Olympic Gold Medalist and a very nice guy. Check out the photo. Al was 300 pounds of muscle. I was not!

As a lifelong student of success and something of a fly-on-the-wall of my life, I absorbed a ton of great success tips from these true super-humans. Time has revealed to me that these folks can teach us a lot about not just sports - but also about life, relationships, and business success. Here are six lessons we can learn from these athletes and others with whom I've shared space.

1. Spend your time around people whom you want to be like.

Why? Superior athletes want to hang around people who are pursuing records and greatness. The environment that is created automatically gives the athlete a much greater chance of successfully reaching his or her own goals. The incredible energy at the Olympic Training Center is something I still feel to this day, even years later. While I was there, I was surrounded by world-class competitors, gold medalists, and other super-achievers. The feeling can drive you to create your personal-best results. Plus, there's a wealth of knowledge surrounding you as well. You can't help but get better.

It's the same in our day-to-day lives. Who are you hanging around? (Think about it.) They either lift you towards your best or hold you down to your lesser self. No relationship is neutral.

2. Keep moving forward to achieve lasting success.

Real success is built over the long-term. These winners have a long-term plan that they follow to get to their best performance in the biggest competitions. They keep moving forward day in and day out. What's your plan for lasting success?

> **"If we strive to be the best we can be each day,
> we can do some wonderful things on this earth."**
> ~ Al Oerter

3. Successes and failures are a part of the process.

These super-achievers know that progress is not an unfettered ascent to the top. Sometimes breakthroughs occur with seemingly little effort. Others times, you may trip and fall back from the pace. None know this better than the great track star Mary Decker Slaney who suffered mishap, tragedy, and misfortune during her incredible career. Despite it all, her greatness as a track legend endures.

Life, business, and relationships do not move in straight lines either. Don't worry when you slip. Just make sure to get back up immediately and go for your goal.

4. Get ready to "do it hard."

When I am scheduled to host a long seminar after landing late via a delayed plane, I never say, "I'm tired, and I don't wanna!" I just do it. It is simply part of the deal. And that attitude ensures my success. Sometimes I, and you, have to do it hard!

Between 1977 and 1987, Edwin Moses won 107 consecutive hurdle finals (122 consecutive races) and set the world record in his event four times. You have to know that there were times during that incredible ten-year run when he didn't feel quite ready to run. It wasn't easy. But, the record shows that against all comers - the world's very best hurdlers who wanted to knock the king off his perch - Edwin "did it hard!"

That's Edwin Moses doing his thing in the photo at right.

Much about life, relationships, and business is not easy. Sometimes, what you want is a hard slog away from you. The key is to make the hard stuff fun by doing what you love to do in your life.

5. Copy those who are doing what you want to do.

The fastest way to gain success is to copy those who are succeeding in their lives. Drop the ego and search-and-reapply the success steps taken by others to your own life.

Reinventing the wheel is a stupid waste of time, energy, and opportunity. From weight loss to growing your business to career success to relationship success to whatever! Model the best examples you can find. (Every one of these world-class athletes studied the competition to uncover some clue that would lead them to better performance.)

6. Find a coach or mentor for faster and better results.

I have trained with, coached, consulted with, interviewed, and worked with some of the top performers in a variety of fields. Olympic athletes. Corporate CEOs. World leaders. Military generals. Fast-growth entrepreneurs. Doctors. Personal development gurus. And on and on. None of them got to where he/she did alone.

> **Believing that you can make it alone is a fatal-conceit that you can't afford.**
> ~ Darryl Mobley

Each of them had a coach or advisor who could walk them through every step of the way from where they were to the accomplishment of their goals. Does this cost money? I hope so! Top-of-their-field experts have a value. But you don't judge a coach on what he/she may cost you. You must look at what they're worth to you. These coaches can accelerate your success accomplishment. Stop struggling personally or in your business and invest in someone to show you the way to your goals - the first time.

Enjoy Life!

Photos in this section: Courtesy of Darryl L. Mobley

Day 16 Action-Steps

Which of the lessons from Olympians will you use in your life?

_____

_____

_____

What are the 3 Key Ideas that you have after reading this day's tips & strategies?

_____

_____

_____

What 2-3 Actions will you take as a result of your Key Ideas (above) and when will you take those actions?

_____

_____

_____

How will you benefit from taking those actions?

_____

_____

_____

DAY 17

You Are Trying To Do Too Much! Just Stop It! How I Dealt With One Woman's Cry For Help.

Let Someone Else Do It

A coaching client of mine called me last week and told me that **she was ready to give up pursuit of her business goals**.

She said that it was all too much and that there was no way that she could do all that it took to achieve her goals.

I listened as she detailed all the stuff she did every day. And it was quite a lengthy list.
Before I go further - a little background: **This woman is extremely talented** and has everything she needs in order to achieve her business goals. I have been working with her in my **BusinessGrowthAce.com** program for about two months and as such, I have a fairly good handle on her potential. Let's just call her "Nancy."

Anyway, I listened to Nancy rant, rave, sob, and complain for about 2-3 minutes regarding how much she had to do every single day. (**I normally don't make it**

past one minute of listening to complaining from anyone except my youngest child. As my youngest, she gets a full 2 minutes!) Unable to stand her whining (valid though it seemed), I interrupted and told Nancy something that rocked her. I told her:

"The President doesn't fly his own plane. Generals don't fight wars by themselves. Quarterbacks don't block for themselves. And queen ants don't forage for the colony's food. Why are you trying to do everything by yourself? This conceit will destroy you. "

She went silent. I wasn't sure if she got my message or if she thought that **I had just gone completely crazy**. (I get that a lot!)

I explained:

"Nancy! You have been trying to fly your own plane, fight the war by yourself, block for yourself, and forage for food. You are trying to do that most difficult of things --- you are trying to do everything yourself. It is impossible. (Except in movies and on TV shows.) You can best grow your business by focusing your efforts on those things that you are great at and that bring in revenue. Everything else should be delegated to someone or something else. <u>If you want to build your business, then you must build your mindset</u>. Build your mindset by getting clear on this: **You can never be incredibly successful following the path of believing that you can do all that "stuff" better than anyone else**. *To take your business to its highest possibility (and have time for family, friends, fun and self), you need to outsource everything,"* that:

- You don't know how to do
- Someone else can do better
- You're not good at
- Takes too much time away from your efforts to attract customers and increase sales
- Someone can do cheaper than your own hourly pay rate

When you delegate/outsource/off-load, you then leverage what you are good at and what can make the most positive difference in your business. This will lead you to making more money and enjoying life a lot more.

I told Nancy much more, and much more specifically.

Nancy "got" what I was saying. She called me back this morning and told me that she had never been more stress-free in her life. She had followed my specific advice for how to properly delegate and how to determine what she should no longer do. And, after just a week of focusing on what she is good at, she had attracted three new clients into her natural health practice. (It normally takes her about six weeks to attract three new clients.) She hasn't implemented everything I told her yet, but she has gotten off to a great start.

I guarantee you that, as with Nancy and my other clients, <u>you can significantly increase your sales and profits when you better leverage your time and focus on to those most-important activities that you are great at</u>, and away from those activities better suited for others. Plus, you will "enjoy life" a whole lot more!

What Gives You Great Value?

The same principles apply in your personal life. Keep your focus and energy on those personal activities that give back the most to your life. What gives great value to your health? What gives great value to your key relationship? What gives great value to your parenting? What gives great value to your mental well-being? What gives you great personal joy? The answers to these questions are where you should put your personal time and effort. Leave everything else to someone else or just don't do the other stuff.

Let me give an example to expand upon this approach to life. Most adults who are in less-than-satisfactory relationships spend more time each week watching TV or surfing online than they do attending to their key relationships. And then they wonder why their relationships blowup in their faces! C'mon! That use (or misuse) of time is clearly self-destructive.

In your business and personal lives, you must decide what is important to you and what you do best that gives you great value. Then, only do those things on that list.

Enjoy Life!

Day 17 Action-Steps

What do you not do well that you will off-load to someone else to do for you?

_____

_____

_____

What are the 3 Key Ideas that you have after reading this day's tips & strategies?

_____

_____

_____

What 2-3 Actions will you take as a result of your Key Ideas (above) and when will you take those actions?

_____

_____

_____

How will you benefit from taking those actions?

_____

_____

_____

DAY 18

What Are You Doing?

The Pet Store and the Squirrel Monkey

When I spoke to my children about how they could best reach their goals in sports and academics, I was reminded of the story about the **pet store and the squirrel monkey**. (*I actually had squirrel monkeys for pets when I was a teenager. My mother once fed scrambled eggs and bacon to my monkeys. It didn't quite work out! But, that's another story for another time!*) Read all of this story because there is a message in it for you.

The Pet Store and The Squirrel Monkey

A man was walking downtown when he passed a pet store. As he looked in the store window, he saw five cages each containing a really **cute squirrel monkey**. He had always liked monkeys so he went into the store.

As he looked at the five little squirrel monkeys, he noticed the **price tags** on the front of their cages. **$75. $75. $75. $75.** And then, **$500.**

He was intrigued by the high price for one of the squirrel monkeys - as they all looked exactly the same to him.

So, he asked the pet store sales clerk **why one of the monkeys**

was priced at $500. The sales clerk told him that particular squirrel monkey could talk. So, it was a bit more expensive than the other "regular" squirrel monkeys.

The man was excited and paid for **that talking squirrel monkey right away.** The clerk took his money, gave him the monkey, and the man took him home.

The next day the man returned to the pet store, found the sales clerk, and told him that the squirrel monkey had not talked yet.

The sales clerk asked the man, "Have you given the squirrel monkey **a multicolored bouncing ball?** He loves to play with the ball."

The man said, "I don't have a multicolored bouncing ball. Can I buy one from you?"

The sales clerk said, "I have one right here that I can sell to you for $21.95."

The man took the ball, paid the clerk, and went back home.

The next day the man returned to the pet store again, found the sales clerk and told him the squirrel monkey still had not said anything.

The sales clerk asked the man, "Have you read to him from **his favorite book, 'Star Monkeys'?** It's a special edition with very nice colored photos and a hand-written note from the author. The talking squirrel monkey loves that book and discusses it after every reading."

The exasperated man said, "I don't have the 'Star Monkeys' book. Can I buy one from you?"

The sales clerk said, "I have the one I read to the talking squirrel monkey right here. It's my only copy, and these books are very rare. But I can sell it to you for just $84.95."

The man glared at the sales clerk, but he took the book, paid the clerk and bustled out the door to go back home.

The very next day the man burst through the door of the pet store, went over to the sales clerk, and yelled at him that **the squirrel monkey was yet to utter a word!**

The sales clerk asked the man, "Is the talking squirrel monkey sitting in his **shiny silver rocking chair?** He just talks up a blue streak whenever he gets to rock in his shiny silver chair. I have the very chair he sat in right here for just $395. That's a discount off the regular price."

The man was furious, but he wanted to see just how far the sales clerk was going to take the talking monkey tale. So, he grabbed the shiny silver chair, signed the credit card charge slip, and sped out the door.

The next day the man returned - looking utterly depressed. He walked slowly back into the pet store carrying the multicolored bouncing ball, the special edition 'Star Monkeys' book, and the shiny silver rocking chair.

The sales clerk saw him and asked, "What's going on? **Didn't the talking squirrel monkey like playing with the multicolored bouncing ball? Didn't he like it when you read to him from his 'Star Monkeys' book? And didn't he enjoy his shiny silver rocking chair?"**

"Yes," the man said. "The talking squirrel monkey **loved playing with the bouncing multicolored ball**. He also seemed to like the **special edition 'Star Monkeys' book** when I read it to him. He even perked up when I gave him the **shiny silver rocking chair**. In fact, the minute I put the rocking chair into the cage with him, he put the multicolored bouncing ball down, closed the special edition 'Star Monkeys' book, sat in the shiny silver rocking chair, and began rocking.

"But then he slumped forward with tears running down his hairy little face - and before he passed away - **the talking squirrel monkey said to me**, *'Don't they sell squirrel monkey food at the pet store?'"*

So what's the message in my little story?

The message is to make sure you are focused on the right things when you try to achieve your goals. It doesn't matter what your goals are – health, business, family, education, relationships, sports, parenting, career – just  make sure you spend your time, money and energy on things that really matter and will lead you to success.

Don't be seduced by shiny, sparkling things or people that will NOT help you achieve your dreams. These things are "dream-stealers." You must master the fundamentals essential to the success you seek.

One of my former football coaches told me that the teams that win most are often the teams that do the best job of **blocking and tackling**. Fancy, trick plays do not lead to consistent winning.

My **college basketball coach** became one of the winningest in the history of the sport. He has been voted coach of the year several times, won multiple national championships, and coached an Olympic team. He taught me that the teams that win most often are the teams that do the best job **rebounding, shooting free throws, and getting the ball in the hands of their best players**. Dunks and fancy passes do not lead to consistent winning. I still remember the time he benched me for taking a long-range jump shot – because I had strayed from the game plan. (I made the shot!)

My **college volleyball coach** is one of the winningest in the history of the sport. He has been voted coach of the year several times. He told me that the teams that win most often are the teams that do the best job **serving consistently and setting the ball to their best spiker**. This coach emphasized – as did each of my other top coaches – that not all players on a team are equal and to pretend they are is a quick way to lose.

One of my **corporate mentors** became a legendary CEO & Chairman of two best-in-class, global companies, and member of the business hall-of-fame. He told me that the companies that win most often in the marketplace are those that best **identify, communicate, and meet consumer desires**.

My coaches were all correct, and these rules can be applied to your life; the most basic things have the biggest impact on personal or professional success or failure.

Blocking; tackling; rebounding; free throw shooting; serving; setting; identifying, communicating, and meeting consumer desires; and getting resources to those best able to use them doesn't seem very sexy. However, focusing on these areas is essential if you want to win. Being great at them requires making decisions as to what is essential and what is dross.

Are you spending your time, efforts, and money on things and people that will generate success to you personally and professionally? Or are you spending time on the shiny, sparkling stuff? Do you know what's really important? Are you able to make tough decisions about what is important and what should be ignored? Are you putting your resources into the hands of your most productive assets? Are you treating your options as if they are all equal?

What are you doing?

Enjoy Life!

Day 18 Action-Steps

What are you spending your time on?

_____

_____

_____

What are the 3 Key Ideas that you have after reading this day's tips & strategies?

_____

_____

_____

What 2-3 Actions will you take as a result of your Key Ideas (above) and when will you take those actions?

_____

_____

_____

How will you benefit from taking those actions?

_____

_____

_____

DAY 19

Want A Better Family & Relationship?

*"We Don't Attract What We Want.
We Attract What We Are."*
~ Darryl L. Mobley

How To Use the Law Of Attraction For Your Family or Relationship

I have done quite a bit of work on evolving an old idea that has a new title. I am speaking of the Law of Attraction. The **Law of Attraction** simply says that **you attract into your life whatever you think about most**. Because you – as all of us – are plugged into the universe, your dominant thoughts will find a way to manifest in your actions and outcomes. I have certainly found this to be true in my personal life and professional endeavors.

Those who are familiar with the Bible will recognize the Law of Attraction and what it represents as a modern spin on these three statements:

- *Therefore I say unto you, All things whatsoever ye pray and ask for, believe that ye receive them, and ye shall have them.*

- *Ask, and it shall be given you; seek, and ye shall find; knock, and it shall be opened unto you.*

- *If thou canst believe, all things are possible to him that believeth.*

My particular interest is in how I, and you, can **apply the Law of Attraction to the important tasks of developing our families and our relationships**. I know that the Law of Attraction works for individuals. But, I became obsessed with peeling away the layers and simplifying how it can be used for the advancement of relationships and families.

I have developed eight simple steps that - when taken - can allow each of us to use the Law of Attraction to take our families and relationships to higher levels. I had 500+ couples/families try these steps. Follow-up research found that each of the couples/families that followed my 8 steps experienced significant improvement in the quality of their relationship with each other, the happiness within their family, the amount of money saved by the family – and in many cases, the grades of the children improved! There were many more benefits experienced by my study participants, too numerous to list here.

I invite you to take the eight steps below and let me know the changes you experience.

My **Law of Attraction For The Family/Relationship** says that your family/relationship will attract whatever the family members collectively dwell on and discuss. Once your family unit/relationship is consciously plugged into the universe, your family's/relationship's goals and dominant thoughts will

eventually appear.

Apply the Law Of Attraction For Your Family (or Relationship) in 8 East Steps

Step 1. Stay alert to the words you and your family (or significant other) use around, about and with, each other. Quite often, our relationships and our families are held captive by our negative and failure-embracing self-talk and our talk with others. One of the absolutely perfect things my parents did while raising me was never say words that limited my dreams. Their words were always positive and empowering when it came to my dreams, goals, or endeavors.

Step 2. Delete the words "Can't," "Won't," "But," and "No" from your discussions. You know the drill: **Change and reframe your words and your thoughts from limitation to limitless.**

Step 3. Develop family (or couple) goals and make sure that every family member gets really clear on the precise things your family has set as goals.

The clearer your goals, the more likely they are to be realized. **Or as my granddad told me many years ago, "Darryl, get to where you can see what you want really well. Then, Grab It!"**

Step 4. Talk with your children (or mate) about their future, their goals, and the possibilities that exist for them. Your words can lift your children (and mate) up above the muck and nonsense of life. And, when your kid (or mate) knows that you believe in them and are a "dream-enabler," the sky is the limit.

Step 5. When you or your significant other are in a negative mood or thought pattern, ask yourselves, **"What do I (or "we" if appropriate) really want?"** Always turn your thoughts toward the goal, the solution, and the future. There you will find a place of happiness and success.

Step 6. Take time at dinner each evening to state appreciation for what the family/relationship does have. It can be comforting to step back from the flames of life and acknowledge the positives you already have.

Step 7. Once each week have your family discuss the action steps each family member will take during the week that will move the family closer to accomplishing the goals established in Step 3 above. Do the same with your mate. **In sports, this would be considered the halftime.** This allows you and your family members to focus your collective and individual thoughts on what you want to attract. You are effectively plugging your entire family into the universe success flow.

Step 8. Write family, relationship and personal goals, dreams, thoughts, successes, questions, progress, discoveries, breakthroughs, insights, plans, challenges, blueprints and lessons-learned in your Life Journal. Refer to this journal each day. My own journal helps keep me and my family focused on positive action, hope and the future.

Do you have personal discipline? I hope so because that is all that stands between you and the lasting and positive benefits of the Law of Attraction for Family & Relationships.

Enjoy Life!

Day 19 Action-Steps

How will you use the Law of Attraction for your family or relationship?

_____

_____

_____

What are the 3 Key Ideas that you have after reading this day's tips & strategies?

_____

_____

_____

What 2-3 Actions will you take as a result of your Key Ideas (above) and when will you take those actions?

_____

_____

_____

How will you benefit from taking those actions?

_____

_____

_____

DAY 20

Does Everything You Touch Turn To Gold?

I Guarantee You More Success If...

Why is it that for some people, it seems as if everything they touch turns to gold? They land the high-paying jobs, they soar in the stock market, and their families and relationships are full of love. For these people, success seems effortless. *What's their secret?*

I am going to share what I've learned from twenty years of life and executive coaching experience. I have coached entrepreneurs, corporate executives, professional and Olympic athletes, military generals, middle school teachers, college professors, college students, business owners, men and women, wealthy and the less-than-wealthy, and everything in between. Many of them are generous in crediting me with helping them reach their goals. In truth, they've taught me a ton about how to succeed. Here's what I've learned:

Unless they won the lottery or inherited a fortune, they've had to work for their financial success just like you. Ditto for success in their personal lives. Success didn't happen overnight. It typically took several years and came after several setbacks.

Successful individuals seek to develop their personal and professional skills – every single day. "Good enough" isn't good enough. "Getting by" doesn't fly. These people are constantly bettering themselves. They learn new business strategies, build stronger personal relationships, and keep their priorities in order and in view.

I have compiled the following seven every-single-day secrets that the successful execute that set them apart from the hoi polloi.

7 Secret Success Tips for Lifelong Success

1. Be confident. Self-confidence affects every aspect of your life. It is that inner voice that tells you, "I can do it!" This voice is the essential motivator that enables you to do things that you might not normally do. I've found that a very small minority of people are self-confident.

2. Don't look back. Always look forward. Don't let past grievances affect your future well-being. There is nothing you can do about your past, so put your energy into attracting and preparing for a successful future.

3. Be optimistic. Choose to be optimistic – no matter the circumstances you encounter. A positive attitude will take you to great heights, wonderful places, new ideas, and fantastic people. A negative attitude delivers you to a living hell.

4. Develop healthy habits. Eating right, drinking lots of water, working out, and getting plenty of sleep will help your body look good and feel great. Then, you will have the energy you need to achieve your goals.

5. Cherish your significant other. If you are fortunate enough to have found your soul mate… I suggest that you love that person with all your heart. Never take your relationship for granted.

6. Schedule "me time." No matter how many appointments, social engagements, or chores you have, set aside at least 60 minutes a day to do something you enjoy. You might enjoy walking, reading, listening to music, playing a guitar… I have been called the "Bulldog of Work-Life Balance," precisely because I make time for me and - as described in the final "secret" below - those I love. I suggest you do the same. Don't let life take from you the real reasons that you live.

7. Make time for friends and family. They are your ultimate support group. Make non-negotiable efforts to spend time with them – or call or write as circumstances require – and let them know how valuable they are to you.

The seven secrets seem simple, don't they? They are. For many, they are so simple as to be easy to avoid doing. Here's my promise to you: When you make these seven secrets your very own, you too will have the Midas touch in all that you do.

Enjoy Life!

Day 20 Action-Steps

Which of the success secrets will you begin using today?

_____

_____

_____

What are the 3 Key Ideas that you have after reading this day's tips & strategies?

_____

_____

_____

What 2-3 Actions will you take as a result of your Key Ideas (above) and when will you take those actions?

_____

_____

_____

How will you benefit from taking those actions?

_____

_____

_____

DAY 21

Your Kids Need Love. It's true!

10 Ways to Give Your Kids the Love They Need

First of all: I have kids. (I'm not one of those folks giving advice about something he's never done.)

Next: My wife and I spend lots of energy and time trying to raise our kids correctly. (You and I know that it's a 24/7/365 job.)

Third: Kids need the love that only parents can give.

Finally: My default is to always give my kids the love they need.

You are with me so far, right? Good.

I believe that the true legacy I leave will be my children. The love I give to, show to, and share with my kids is the key to my legacy being a good one. I hope you agree.

A listener to my radio show wrote to tell me that she heard me say that children are "need-machines 24/7/365." I said it and I know it to be 100% true! Your kids need your love if they are to grow up balanced and ready to win at the game of life. (They also need your money, but that's a different discussion.)

I am a life or executive coach to many parents. I also work with hundreds of teenagers in my "Life Coaching for Teens" program. The number 1 question I am asked about parenting can be summed up as follows: "How can I change my child's behavior?" Of course, the specific answer has to do with the specific change desired. My answer to the question always includes encouraging parents to give their kids more love. (Why give your kids more love? Because it works.)

Most parents respond to my request to give more love by asking, "How can I give my kid any more love than I already do?"

My answer to that question is really two answers.

My first answer is that we, as parents, must work non-stop at giving love to our kids. Is it tiring dealing with a headstrong teenager? Is the average teenager a hardhead? Do you fret when your child repeats non-productive behavior despite your best advice? Are there other things in your life that drain your energy, leaving little for your kids? Yes. Yes. Yes. And, yes. It is what it is. But this I know to be true: we must not tire out before we send our kids off into adulthood. This may mean that we have to outlast our kids' resolve to ignore us.

My second answer is that we must use every tool available to give love to our kids. Yes. I said, "tool." Building a child into a capable adult is similar to building a house. As in a house – so too with raising kids – you need to create the foundation, the structure, the internal wiring, the roof & walls for protection against life's elements, and so on. Clearly, it takes more than one tool to build a complete house. It's the same way when it comes to building your kid. You need different tools to use while parenting. I've identified ten tools for giving love to kids. They have delivered great results for the parents I coach.

10 Ways to Give Your Kids The Love They Need.

1. Operate on the principle that **children will do ninety percent of what they see, but just ten percent of what they are told**. You must lead and love them in word and deed. I surprise myself when I find that I am doing something that my dad did 40 years ago, even though he never told me to do it.

2. **Read to your child every day.** In addition, when the time is right, have your kids read to you. Yes – that includes teenagers. If your kid is old enough to see an advertisement and then hound you with all the reasons why they just must have whatever it was that they saw, then they are not too old to read to you from one of the great books, a college website, a business magazine, a school book, or wherever! When you and your child read to each other you are loving through the sharing of information.

3. **Keep school projects and gifts given to you by your child, and proudly display the new ones you are given**. This showing of love will pay dividends for eternity.

4. **Don't give your child every new gadget that comes down the pike**. Give them the love of delayed gratification and learning to do without. Too many of us give our children virtually every toy, piece of technology, or other treat they want. Then we wonder why our kids know the "cost of everything, but the value of nothing." This is the reason why so many of the children of those of us in the middle-class and beyond are soft and will be easy prey later-in-life for the hungry-for-success, hardworking, less-pampered kid who had to do more with much less.

5. I have teenagers and this I know: **Even when your children think they know it all, they still want you around**, if only hanging invisibly in the background. They need you to help them navigate the tough waters of "growing up." In an episode of my TV talk show, I interviewed teens and this very opinionated and in-a-hurry-to-grow-up 15-year-old boy told me that he wanted his father to tell him the hard truths about life – even when he (the boy) acted as if he didn't want to hear it. One teenage girl opined that, "I can't learn how to win at life when I'm an adult unless my parents keep telling me stuff, even when I tell them that I don't want to hear it. They should just keep on telling me what they think I should know."

6. **Tell your children that you love them at every opportunity**. In the morning. With handwritten notes. Via the phone. During dinner. Before their heads hit their pillows at night. Be relentless in letting your children know that you love them even when they act as if they are too grown-up to listen to you.

7. **Get involved with your kids' extracurricular activities**. As much as possible, don't just drop your kids off at events and activities. Your presence benefits your children because they know that you are interested in what they do. It also benefits you because there are few things more enjoyable or memorable than watching your kids in competitive or other engaging situations. Being present is love in action. Be sure and take a camera with you!

8. **Teach the reality of consequences**. Let your children know upfront what you expect from them and the consequences for improper behavior. Consistently follow through on your consequences, or your children will learn that they can do whatever they want, and nothing will happen to them. The problem with this is that real life dropkicks those who never

learn that bad behavior leads to tough consequences. Getting your kids to understand that there are consequences for everything they do is one of the best ways to show your love.

9. **Engage your children in discussions about their day's school activities and other events**. Ask them about their day. (Dinner is a great time for this.) Share what happened in your day. The key to the relationship with your child is communication. You'll need to talk (lots!) and listen (lots!). Be aware that your kids are a jumble of emotions with fleeting smidgens of common sense. That means that they may not always be able to say properly what they mean or say it correctly. The love that is at the core of your discussions with your children will be remembered and valued by you and your kids long after your hair has turned gray, and the college loans are paid off.

10. **Hug your children each and every morning before they leave for school.** By definition, we love what we hug. (Think about that one!) Hugging – the physical communication of your love – can be just the thing to keep your kid moving in the right direction and making the right choices.

There! Ten tools you can use immediately. Now go ahead and build your (almost) perfect child.

Enjoy Life!

Day 21 Action-Steps

What will you do today to make your child just a little more perfect?

_____

_____

_____

What are the 3 Key Ideas that you have after reading this day's tips & strategies?

_____

_____

_____

What 2-3 Actions will you take as a result of your Key Ideas (above) and when will you take those actions?

_____

_____

_____

How will you benefit from taking those actions?

_____

_____

_____

DAY 22

Are You Settling? Or, Are You Living?

Don't Back Down!

Here we are. The economy is in either flux (if you're optimistic) or freefall (if you're a bit less optimistic). Change is all around us. We know that we need to do more - often with fewer resources. **Everything says that we should just, "be happy with what we have."** For many, life up until now has been one of settling for the safe, the secure, and the certain. **Many think that they shouldn't shoot for the moon since they probably won't get there. I mean, we're getting older and we should not go after that big, hairy goal of ours. And we should not be too picky about our relationship because we probably can't do better.** How's all of this sound to you?

Let me tell you that all of this pressure to settle for less than living at the highest level is a self-defeating illusion. The illusion is fueled by a variety of fears. Fear to dream. Fear of rejection. Fear of success. Fear of the unknown. Fear of the change required. Fear of what others will say. Fear of the future. **F.E.A.R.**

FEAR is most often just...

F.alse
E.vidence
A.ppearing
R.eal

Fear has only the power you give it.

I implore you: <u>Don't embrace your fears. Embrace your possibilities!</u>

You must stop settling for less than your best. You must instead focus on what it will feel like when you "go for it!" and when you get it! If anything, now is the time to look life right in the eye and demand what you want.

Here are **four powerful Action-Steps that you can take to Live instead of Settle**:

Step 1. Write down what you DEMAND from life. Note - your list is actually a DEMAND you are making of yourself.

Step 2. Next to each DEMAND write down what your life will be like if you continue to settle for less than your very best. Then write down what your life would be like - what is the best thing that will happen - when you fully apply yourself to going for your very best life goals.

Step 3. Write down a list of the very short list of people who can be resources to you as you move forward towards your highest possibilities. These are the folks who support you in your dream pursuit. Let these folks know what you plan to do, and why! If they are worth anything they will assist you with their ideas, experiences, and other resources. What should you do if you don't have anyone in your life who can be a resource for you? Jump to step four below. You should not back off from going for your best life just because you may stand alone. All successful people have had to stand alone - at some point in time - as they pursued their giant selves.

Step 4. Put together the best plan you can for getting what you DEMAND from life. Then, get busy. Start taking massive action steps immediately that will lead you to what you DEMAND from life and from yourself! Do what you were put here to do!

Enjoy Life!

Day 22 Action-Steps

What do you demand from life?

_____

_____

_____

What are the 3 Key Ideas that you have after reading this day's tips & strategies?

_____

_____

_____

What 2-3 Actions will you take as a result of your Key Ideas (above) and when will you take those actions?

_____

_____

_____

How will you benefit from taking those actions?

_____

_____

_____

DAY 23

Is Your Life in Balance or Out of Control?

14 Things You Absolutely Must Do to Get Work-Life Balance

Life is sweetest when lived in balance. That's my story, and I'm sticking to it!

For the past twenty years I've conducted research among those who feel that their lives are balanced, and those who believe that their lives are way out of whack. I have seen that those in balance and those out of balance are not separated by education, upbringing, marital status, or even income. What separates them? Here's the short answer: the actions they take day in and day out.

What I share with you below are 14 of the actions taken by those who enjoy the benefits of work-life balance. How powerful are these actions? They are used by my most successful life-coaching clients. Trust me. They work.

14 Steps That Will Get You Work-Life Balance

1. Write down the 100 things you want to do, be, have or experience during your time on this earth. Dream big. When you finish this list, you will be focused and more energized about each day of your life.

2. Develop your vision book. A vision book is a special book you create that contains words, pictures/images, and other stuff that represents a visualization of the life you seek to live. Did you know that your brain will work 24/7 for you and attempt to achieve everything contained in your subconscious mind? The key to leveraging this amazing subconscious brainpower is to keep vivid images of what you want your life to be constantly fresh in your "mind's eye." Your vision book does this for you. Your Vision Book will balance your every day and keep you focused on the life you want to live.

3. Decide who you love. Carve out time each day to let that person - or those people - know how you feel about them.

4. Decide your 10 major Life Goals. Keep the list with you always and refer to it frequently. You will then find it easier to stay on track and be happy with the track that you're on.

5. Limit your TV watching, tweeting, texting, facebooking, and so on. These activities - with few exceptions - take away your energy, your time, your initiative, and your engagement with real life. Surely you have more important things to do in your life than be a slave to technology? Studies show that kids who spend lots of time tweeting, texting, facebooking, and watching TV make much poorer grades than kids who spend little time doing these activities. Why would these activities have any less negative an impact on your life?

6. Keep a Journal so that you document the people, places, things, goals, and activities that are important to you. You should also keep a tally of the challenges you face, along with your successes, wins, losses, learnings, strategies, and resources. This will become one of your most important assets.

7. Do something that you find "FUN!" at least once a week.

8. Carve out time - on at least 3 days a week - to exercise. All you need is 30 minutes of activity to make a huge difference in your fitness, your health, and your quality of life.

9. When facing competing demands, ask yourself: What's the cost to me? Which one will move me closer to my life goals? Your answer will tell you which one to choose.

10. Let go of the Dream Stealers (people, things, habits, etc.) that are holding you back from achieving your goals. You cannot soar like an eagle if you hang with the turkeys and vultures that disable your attempts to make progress.

11. Stop any activities you currently take part in that are non-priorities.

12. Focus on the Important Things In Your Life. What things are you unwilling to die having left undone?

13. Call two friends every weekend. You will stay connected and build the ties that last forever. These relationships are good for your heart - in more ways than one.

14. Join a Mastermind group that will encourage you in your quest for work-life balance. Such a group will keep you honest and hold you to a high standard.

What I've observed is that people get so caught up in work that they forget to live a full life. **That - to me - is unacceptable.** I promise you that when you up-level your life with the 14 action-steps above, you will get the following benefits that flow from work-life balance:

- You will attract more positive people and opportunities in your life.
- You will become passionate about your family & key relationship, your friendships, your career, and YOU!
- You will become a master at making time work for you so that you do more and better work in less time.

Enjoy Life!

Day 23 Action-Steps

What will you do today to get your life back in balance?

_____

_____

_____

What are the 3 Key Ideas that you have after reading this day's tips & strategies?

_____

_____

_____

What 2-3 Actions will you take as a result of your Key Ideas (above) and when will you take those actions?

_____

_____

_____

How will you benefit from taking those actions?

_____

_____

_____

DAY 24

Any Snakes In Your Life?

The Legend of the Snake and the Man

A friend of mine called me the other day and told me that his Mom told him that she was helping one of his cousins. My friend told me that this fully-grown cousin had a long background as a crime-involved, drug taking, non-working, lying, no-account, you-can't-trust-him idiot. His advice to his Mom was to not get involved with this cousin. Of course – she ignored his advice.

Since I also have a relative or two who may be just like my friend's cousin, I could not help but think of <u>the story of the Man and the Snake</u>. Maybe you can relate - -

A man was walking up a mountain when he heard a voice from the bushes.

"Carry me with you," the voice said. The man turned and saw that it was a snake speaking to him.

The man protested, "You are a snake. If I carry you up the mountain, you will bite me."

Got Snakes?

"I wouldn't do that," the snake assured. "All I need is some help. I am slow, and you are fast, please be kind and carry me to the top of the mountain."

It was against his better judgment, but the man agreed. He picked up the snake, put him in his shirt, and resumed the journey. When they reached the top, he reached in his shirt to remove the snake, and the snake bit him!

Do you trust snakes?

The man fell to the ground, dying from the snake's poison, and the snake slithered away.

"You lied!" the man cried out as he lay on the ground in pain, "You said you wouldn't bite me."

The snake stopped and looked back, "Of course I lied! You knew who I was when you picked me up. I'm a snake!"

We hear the legend and shake our heads. The man should have known better, we bemoan. And we are right. He should have.

And so should we. But don't we often do the same? Don't we believe the lies of the snakes in our life? Don't we pick up what we should leave alone? Aren't we hanging around some folks who don't make a positive difference in our life? Don't we hold tight to the bad habits that hold us back? Don't we engage in too many negative conversations with those who specialize in everything-sucks thinking?

If you trust snakes, you will be bitten!

If you want to reach your goals, you must not carry snakes with you during your life journey. Snakes will bite you, sap your energy, diffuse your focus, screw you up in so many ways, and keep you from Living Your BEST Life and reaching your Goals.

Enjoy Life!

Day 24 Action-Steps

Which snakes will you stop carrying in your life??

_____

_____

_____

What are the 3 Key Ideas that you have after reading this day's tips & strategies?

_____

_____

_____

What 2-3 Actions will you take as a result of your Key Ideas (above) and when will you take those actions?

_____

_____

_____

How will you benefit from taking those actions?

_____

_____

_____

DAY 25

What is the First Step To Success?

"What is the first step to success?"

I am asked this question or some version of it almost every day.

My answer is always the same. Sometimes that answer energizes the person who asked the question. Sometimes the answer scares the person. Sometimes it angers.

No matter. The answer doesn't change.

The first step to success is **taking responsibility for everything about your life.**

For many, this is very difficult to accept. No matter. The answer doesn't change.

You are responsible for the life you live.

What you have done or not done has created your reality. Your actions or inaction have determined the quality of your relationships, the amount of money you make, where you live, your weight, your job, your education, your personal debt, your health, the behavior of your children, and your destiny.

You know it's true. Sometimes we try to convince ourselves that forces outside of ourselves are the cause of our shortcomings. I think that I've heard it all: I smoke because I'm on a diet. I am overweight because of stress. I live here because I'm near family. I'm unhappy because of my boyfriend. My kids fell prey to peer pressure. My boss has it out for me. The "man" won't let me get ahead. And on and on and on. If it's negative, it must be something or someone else's fault. If it's positive, we tend to grab all the credit. You may have heard the saying:

"Failure is an orphan. Success has many fathers."

Outside forces do not control your destiny. YOU control your destiny - and the here and now - 100%.

The power is in accepting total responsibility.

Let's take a different look at this.

"If you want to Live Your Best Life, you must take total responsibility and decide to commit yourself to creating winning thoughts, actions, habits, skills and goals."

Let's say that you don't like your ballooning weight. Your weight is not the fault of your kids, your job requirements, how much you travel, or the baby you had two years ago. Your heaviness is a result of what you choose to put in your mouth and how often you choose to exercise. If you accept this reality, then you can take charge of your weight. Taking charge might include adding 15 minutes of walking to your daily schedule. Or, you might adjust what you eat, how much, and when you eat.

Let's say that your business sales and profits are not where you want them to be. This is not something that you can simply blame on the economy and leave it at that. Your company's marketing, level of innovation, sales staff quality & selling efforts, and the relevance of what you have to offer to customers determine your business sales and profits. Some of the greatest companies in the history of the world were started during times of economic distress. If you accept these facts, then you can take your sales and profits to new heights by taking powerful business-growth actions to best meet customer needs and outperform competition.

Let's say that you are not satisfied with your life. The sour attitude you have about your circumstances is not caused by the weather, your neighborhood, government, spouse, kids, boss, ex, job, or in-laws. Your sour attitude is a result of what you choose to think, read, do, or listen to, and with whom you choose to do what you do. If you accept this reality, you can then make the changes needed to create the life of your dreams.

You may choose to re-program your thinking by reading and listening to personal development books and audio programs. (I have read some 3,000+ books on personal development and I am sure that my thinking has been dramatically enhanced by this activity of choice.) You may need to up-level your parenting skills so that you help your kids achieve enhanced outcomes. You may need to re-calibrate your relationship skills so that you can move your marriage or dating situation to a better place, or get out altogether. You may need to get your butt into a job you can feel good about.

I also encourage you to take strength from what's good in your life. We all have positives to take from aspects of our lives.

That said, stomp out the habit of complaining and blaming others for what you have – or don't have – in your life. This is a key to you moving towards your best destiny.

What you take responsibility for – you can then expand, create, or delete from your life. Success, failure, good times, bad times, mistakes, happiness, and unhappiness are all within your hands. You will do great things. You may also really screw up. No matter. It's all on you! If you are in a bad position, get out! If you've made a mistake, correct it right now!

Taking responsibility represents immense power.

Here's how you use your immense power:

1. You must BELIEVE in your power.

2. Don't give up your power. You are your own magic genie. You are your own King/Queen. You are the ruler of your destiny.

3. Demand (of yourself) total responsibility for your results.

4. Don't blame others and don't complain about where you are. This is negative energy that won't improve your circumstances.

5. Assess where you are. Face the truth. <u>Make the changes</u> you need to make. If others don't support your desire to improve your situation, do what former-slave-turned-conductor-of-the-underground-railroad Harriet Tubman did when she first escaped to freedom from slavery and her brothers turned back due to fear ---- move on without them.

6. <u>Ask</u> for what you need. **<u>Seek</u>** what you want. **<u>Knock</u>** to open the doors to your better destiny.

> "Your life does not get better by chance, it gets better by change."
> ~ Darryl L. Mobley

<u>You are your own Superman/Wonder Woman</u> because you are now in tune with **Taking Responsibility and Taking Action**. Taking responsibility and taking action – together – represent the greatest power of them all. It's all on YOU!

Enjoy Life!

Day 25 Action-Steps

What have you not been taking responsibility for in your life?

_____

_____

_____

What are the 3 Key Ideas that you have after reading this day's tips & strategies?

_____

_____

_____

What 2-3 Actions will you take as a result of your Key Ideas (above) and when will you take those actions?

_____

_____

_____

How will you benefit from taking those actions?

_____

_____

_____

DAY 26

The Answer To This Question Determines Your Destiny

Are You A Hedgehog or A Fox?

Has anyone ever asked you this question? Probably not. Well, that's why I'm here.

I was recently speaking with my great friend Sheldon, who turned me on to "the hedgehog and the fox." The core of this discussion was driven by the famous essay, "The Hedgehog and the Fox," by Sir Isaiah Berlin in which he divided the world's people into hedgehogs and foxes, based upon an ancient Greek parable: "The fox knows many things, but the hedgehog knows one big thing."

Jim Collins covers the idea fully in his best-selling book, Good to Great, as follows:

"The fox is a cunning creature, able to devise a myriad of complex strategies for sneak attacks upon the hedgehog. Day in and day out, the fox circles around the hedgehog's den, waiting for the perfect moment to pounce. Fast, sleek, beautiful, fleet of foot, and crafty—the fox looks like the sure winner. The hedgehog, on the other hand, is a dowdier creature, looking like a genetic mix-up between a porcupine and a small armadillo. He waddles along, going about his simple day, searching for lunch, and taking care of his home.

The fox waits in cunning silence at the juncture in the trail. The hedgehog, minding his own business, wanders right into the path of the fox. "Aha, I've got you now!" thinks the fox. He leaps out, bounding across the ground, lightning fast. The little hedgehog, sensing danger, looks up and thinks, "Here we go again. Will he ever learn?" Rolling up into a perfect little ball, the hedgehog becomes a sphere of sharp spikes, pointing outward in all directions. The fox, bounding toward his prey, sees the hedgehog defense and calls off the attack. Retreating to the forest, the fox begins to calculate a new line of attack. Each day, some version of this battle between the hedgehog and the fox takes place, and despite the greater cunning of the fox, the hedgehog always wins."

Why does the hedgehog win the battle with the fox? Because the hedgehog does its one big thing very, very well. In the case of the hedgehog, it rolls up into a ball and waits the fox out. The fox, on the other hand, wastes its time in a battle in which it cannot be the best.

The hedgehog is very focused on what it can be the best at. That being, rolling up into a ball of defense. The fox is out there with its superior quickness, speed, cunning, strength, beauty, and ability to plan – but without superior focus.

Here's the basic Hedgehog Concept as expressed by Jim Collins: A Hedgehog Concept is not a goal to be the best, a strategy to be the best, an intention to be the best, a plan to be the best. It is an understanding of what you can be the best at. The distinction is crucial. According to Collins, the people who build great companies are, more or less, hedgehogs. They use their inner hedgehog to create the Hedgehog Concept for their companies. Those who build companies that are not as successful tend to be foxes, never beating the hedgehog and instead suffering from scatteration and inconsistency.

I also know that the people who build great relationships and families are very much like hedgehogs. But, let me continue…

We all have the choice as to how we will approach life – as hedgehogs or foxes. I am not here to suggest which approach you should choose. I will say to you that if you live your life based on what you can be the best at, you may achieve more success than you thought possible.

I am working to apply the Hedgehog Concept to my business life. I know that Life and Executive Coaching is one of the things that I can be best at. But, there is more to gaining full advantage from this concept than just this. You must dig a bit deeper. How so?

There are three questions you must ask yourself if you wish to call up your inner hedgehog.

1. *What can I be the best in the world at?* I don't mean being merely competent. Also note that what you could be the best at may not be something you are currently doing as a job.

2. *What can I make lots of money doing?*

3. *What am I deeply passionate about?* The idea here is to uncover what makes you passionate.

To the extent that you have the same answer to each of the three questions, you can be extremely successful – even great!

So, what will it be for you? Hedgehog or fox?

Make it a point to apply what I've shared with you about the hedgehog and the fox before your head hits the pillow tonight.

Enjoy Life!

Day 26 Action-Steps

What can you be among the best at doing?

_____

_____

What are the 3 Key Ideas that you have after reading this day's tips & strategies?

_____

_____

_____

What 2-3 Actions will you take as a result of your Key Ideas (above) and when will you take those actions?

_____

_____

_____

How will you benefit from taking those actions?

_____

_____

_____

DAY 27

Is Your Family Aggravating You?

Are Your Kids Out of Control?

What's Up with Your Spouse?

Does It Feel As If Every One In Your Family Has Their Own Selfish Agenda?

Some years ago, a very well-known female celebrity called me up and bluntly said that she needed me to coach her and her family. She said that her family was way out of control. Her kids seemed to be doing everything they could to cause agitation. Her husband had become more like a roommate than a loving spouse. (There was very little intimacy between them anymore.)

She felt that she was unable to successfully keep her focus on both her demanding career and the needs of her family. It seemed to her that everyone in her home was "just doing his or her own thing." She felt stressed. She felt like a failure. She felt as if her family was not a real "family." She asked me to help. Let's call her "Ms. X."

After more than an hour of questioning Ms. X, I felt as if I there were some obvious areas to address that could make a real and almost immediate difference for this woman and her family. When I told her that I thought I could help her, she seemed to start breathing again. (Always a good thing!)

One area we worked on was **getting everyone in her household aligned.** I knew that none of the problems Ms. X identified would be solved until her family started acting as a team. What follows is the approach I used to successfully get her family on the right track. Spoiler Alert! Yes. Ms. X's children became problem <u>solvers</u> instead of problem <u>causers</u>. They became far more focused. Yes. Ms. X and her husband rekindled their relationship. Yes. Ms. X felt far less stress in her role as parent and spouse. Yes. Ms. X began to feel as if she was a good mom. Yes. Ms. X began to enjoy her career.

G.O.A.L.S. Are Guaranteed to Get Your Family Pulling in the Same Direction

It can be challenging getting children to see beyond their current situation. Why should we expect the typical 8, 12, 15 (or whatever) year old to focus on something that might happen six months, 12 months, or 5 years from now when that forward period of time represents such a large percentage of their current age? That's a fairly difficult task - even for many adults!

After lots of trial & error, I developed a way to get kids to look out 3, 6 or even 12 months. I call it my G.O.A.L.S. exercise. I tried it out on my kids for the first time several years ago, and it worked beautifully. They became focused on the future, and they became aligned with the family unit as a whole. I saw that they achieved more, were happier, had a better outlook on their young lives, and functioned as part of a smoothly operating family unit. And now, most of my clients are using it to benefit their kids and families.

The key to my G.O.A.L.S. exercise is to do it when the entire family is together, and there's nothing to break the concentration. We do the G.O.A.L.S. exercise every three months – either over dinner or Saturday lunch or when we are all in the car on a road trip. (There is absolutely no escaping from my car during this exercise because I set the driver's lock system to stun!) This focused "family" time is the perfect environment in which to grow new ideas for the family unit and break through any barriers that may be present.

Another benefit to my G.O.A.L.S. exercise is that it gets the entire family pulling in the same direction and invested in the individual success of each family member.

In addition, you will become closer to each member of your family, and they will become closer to you. You will learn how they think. They will gain the advantage of observing your thinking.

Darryl's G.O.A.L.S. Exercise

> *Let me tell you upfront that this works best if you have one of your kids write down the ideas and answers for each of the steps. The involvement of your child is key to getting maximum impact from this exercise.*

The first five steps to my G.O.A.L.S. Exercise are expressed using the letters in the word "GOALS."

G - What do we want to "get" as a family?
O - What do we want to "observe" (see) as a family?
A - What do we want to "attract" into the family (using the Law of Attraction)?
L - What do we want to "learn" as a family?
S - What empowering words will we "say" to each other?

Step 1 - Ask each family member - **What do we want to "get" as a family over the next 3 months?** Come to some agreement as to the 2, 3, or even ten key things you want as a family over the next three months. (You may select any time period that meets your needs.) You may want to "get" a DVD that you all can watch together. Or, perhaps someone will want the family to "get" information on that cruise that you've all been talking about going on forever. You may all resolve to "get" into shape. Or anything else that strikes your fancy.

Tip: Encourage each family member to make suggestions.

Step 2 - Ask each family member - **What do we want to "observe" (see) as a family over the next three months?** Same process as Step 1. You may want to "see" a movie together. Or, perhaps you can go to "see" your child's teacher. A sunset. A rodeo. Again - let the sky be the limit.

Tip: Make sure that the conversation is not full of negative comments that stop communication dead. Examples: "That's stupid." "I don't like that." "Are you out of your f#$^%% mind?!!!"

Step 3 - Ask each family member - **What do we want to "attract" into the family (using the Law of Attraction) over**

the next three months? Same process as Step 1. Simply put - Your family can attract those things which represent your family's dominant thoughts and which reflect your family's dominant actions.

Tip: The key to this working for your family is the investment of each member in the thoughts and actions that can attract what you all wish.

Step 4 - Ask each family member - **What do we want to "learn" as a family over the next three months?** Same process as Step 1. You may want to learn a line dance together. Or, you might want to learn more about growth stocks. Some want to learn more about a new business that has been discussed by the kids. One time, my family decided that we wanted to learn all of the key health measurements for each family member. My kids were particularly fired up to learn our blood pressures, cholesterol readings, PSA readings, and so on. It was great! (There's nothing quite like having your kids keep an eye on what you eat and how much you exercise.)

Tip: Don't underestimate your kids just because they are young. Even those below the age of ten can surprise you with their contributions to this exercise.

Step 5 - Ask each family member - **Which empowering words will we "say" to each other over the next three months?** Same process as Step 1. The truth is that this step may do more to uplift your family than any other single thing you do. Here is my turnabout on the old childhood rhyme:

"Sticks and stones may break my bones. But the positive words spoken to me by those close to me can keep me strong and protect me against anything life may throw at me."

Come up with a list of words and sayings that each member of your family will say to each other each day.

Tip: Say the words to your significant other and to your kids in the morning, at noon and at night.

Step 6 - Now that all of the answers have been written down for each step, decide as a family – for each step – which **ideas you will commit to as a family**. Then, develop the specific action steps each family member will take to do each and everything that was committed to.

Complete all six steps and you will bring your family members closer together, accomplish more individually and as a family unit, bring more happiness into your life, and teach your kids how to dream and pursue goals.

Try it and let me know how it works for you.

Enjoy Life!

Day 27 Action-Steps

What great joy will surround your family once all get on the same boat?

_____

_____

_____

What are the 3 Key Ideas that you have after reading this day's tips & strategies?

_____

_____

_____

What 2-3 Actions will you take as a result of your Key Ideas (above) and when will you take those actions?

_____

_____

_____

How will you benefit from taking those actions?

_____

_____

_____

DAY 28

Do You Have A 'To-Don't' List?

We Are What We Do.
That Makes Life Easy.

I am a huge proponent of To-Do Lists. I know from research and my personal experience that regular use of a To-Do List will accelerate the journey to success and goal accomplishment. I can look at your To-Do Lists over time and find out everything I need to know in order to predict your destiny.

However, as a life and executive coach I've learned that just as important as what you do is what you don't do. Let's look at a simple example:

There are two healthy women. They are substantially the same age, body type, height, and weight. They attended the same college. They eat the same types of foods. Both of them are ambitious. They are at the same level in the same company. They both decide to enter a marathon a year from now. They both want to do well in running the marathon. Over the next year, here's what they do:

Woman A	Woman B
Develops a marathon training plan	Develops a marathon training plan
Purchases marathon training shoes	Purchases marathon training shoes
Eats foods that provide the energy needed for marathon	Eats foods that provide the energy needed for marathon
Goes on training runs every day according to schedule	Procrastinates and only goes on training runs once a week or so

As we scan the lists of what both women did to prepare for the marathon, we can see that they both developed a training plan, purchased the right equipment, and ate the right foods. The key difference in their preparation is that Woman B did procrastinate whereas Woman A did train every day. Based on the key difference in what they did, we should expect that Woman A will perform better in the marathon than Woman B.

This little example is a reflection of what each of us can expect to get from our choices regarding what we do and what we don't do. Said another way, we have to do the right things and not do those things that hamper us.

That is why I have developed a list of things you should not do. I want you to send me an email and request my one-month list of **what you should NOT do**. Print off the one-pager and refer to it often. Turn the list I share with you into habits and your life will be uplifted dramatically. I guarantee it.

Send your request to:

Hello@CoachMobley.com

Enjoy Life!

Day 28 Action-Steps

What will you stop doing so that you can live the life you want?

_____

_____

_____

What are the 3 Key Ideas that you have after reading this day's tips & strategies?

_____

_____

_____

What 2-3 Actions will you take as a result of your Key Ideas (above) and when will you take those actions?

_____

_____

_____

How will you benefit from taking those actions?

_____

_____

_____

DAY 29

Do You Have A Plan B?

What To Do When Your Plan A Doesn't Work

During these tumultuous times, I am reminded that it is always good to have a well-thought-out Plan B. Why?

Because sometimes *Plan B* is better than your *Plan A*.

The life I now live is a Plan B.

Several years ago, I did quite a bit of marketing and strategy consulting for major corporations. It was great work. I truly enjoyed helping clients increase their sales, market share and profits. I got a thrill out of working to uncover breakthroughs that allowed my clients to win in the marketplace. I made a lot of money (because companies will always pay those who can help them sell more at a greater profit). I also traveled constantly on business for my clients to every big city in the U.S. and Internationally. From San Francisco to Miami, Mexico City to London, Seoul to Rome, Rio to Chicago, Hong Kong to Toronto, and every place in between. The food was great. The clients were great. My wife and I traveled together for virtually all of this. It was "all good."

Then my wife and I got pregnant with our first child. (Shazam! How did that happen? **Blame it on Rio**.) Anyway, I decided that I did not want to miss the birth of my child or spend all of my time on the road while my child was growing up.

My bottom line: I was unwilling to succeed professionally and fail personally. The Internet is great, but I really did not want to have to be emailed a picture of my child's first steps, first words, and so on. Quite simply, this meant that **I needed to do something that would replace the income from my Plan A endeavors**.

So, I asked myself a powerful question. I asked myself, **"What would I do to reach my goals if I stopped doing what I'm doing right now?"** The answers I came up with have made all the difference. The answers became my **Powerful Plan B**.

Among other things, as part of my Powerful Plan B **I decided to expand my Life Coaching and Executive Coaching business as a way to make up for the income I was giving up because I no longer wanted to travel non-stop for the marketing and strategy business**. I decided to coach only those clients who were fully committed to becoming more successful. I now do most of my work via the Internet and phone, and my traveling is much more controlled. That's a good thing because I now have clients living on six of the seven continents.

I still speak professionally to organizations that want my particular truth and at colleges, and I do a bit of consulting on marketing/strategy in certain situations. My entire family (including the first child and the knuckleheads that followed) has traveled with me on my business trips to Japan, Germany, Switzerland, Mexico, Hawaii, London, Paris, Italy, Monaco, Canada, and all over the U.S. My **Powerful Plan B** business allows me the freedom to travel when I choose and with those I love the most.

All I can say is "Wow!" I am very happy with the life that moving to my **Powerful Plan B** has allowed me to create. My relationships with my children and wife are over-the-top good. My life experiences (as a horse whisperer, snake wrangler, fruit picker, hog slopper, Army

Officer, corporate executive, entrepreneur, Co-founder of Beauty Of The Nile, parachutist, marketing/strategy consultant, Life & Executive Coach, corporate trainer, and father & husband) and extensive study have allowed me to <u>develop a proven approach to helping others succeed personally and professionally</u>. **None of this would have happened had I stayed with my Plan A.** (Come to think of it, perhaps I am on Plan <u>N</u> at this point!)

What's So Good About Your Plan A?

Couldn't I have made the change to this better life even earlier? I don't want to think about what I'd be doing if I had never asked myself the **Powerful Plan B** question. Let's flip the script. What if I had asked myself the **Powerful Plan B** question five years earlier: **"What would I do to reach my goals if I stopped doing what I'm doing right now?"**

You don't need to make the mistake I made by waiting too long to switch to my Powerful Plan B.

What is your Powerful Plan B? What would you do to reach your goals if you stopped doing what you're doing right now?

Make A List

Here's what I want you to do: Make a list of the top 5 things you currently do professionally and personally, more or less by habit. The list might include how you run your business, how you interact with your significant other, what you eat, how you earn money, and so on. Then, ask yourself the **Powerful Plan B** question about each of them. Your answers may lead you to your castle in the sky.

In truth, the **Powerful Plan B question** (and your answer) might be the most valuable thing I ever share with you. I have lived it and I know it can significantly up-level your life in every area that is important to you.

Enjoy Life!

Day 29 Action-Steps

What's your Plan B?

_____

_____

What are the 3 Key Ideas that you have after reading this day's tips & strategies?

_____

_____

_____

What 2-3 Actions will you take as a result of your Key Ideas (above) and when will you take those actions?

_____

_____

_____

How will you benefit from taking those actions?

_____

_____

_____

DAY 30

What Should You Do When Times Are Tough?

"The way I see it, if you want the rainbow,
you gotta put up with the rain."
Dolly Parton

Check out what I wrote for you on the next page.

THE STRUGGLE MAKES YOU GREAT

When times are tough, as you know they are,
And every goal you seek seems so very far;

When all you want is to be your best,
But these challenging times are giving you a stern test;

When the success you crave seems out of touch,
And your thirst for it almost hurts too much;

When the light in the tunnel might again be a train,
And you're wondering if you can endure more pain;

Now is the time to resolve and realize,
That the life you want is indeed a huge prize;

Because every great prize comes at great cost,
Nothing great is gained unless there is also great loss;

Yes - it is now that you will step up your champion's gait,
Press on to your goal because it is the struggle that makes you great!
~ Darryl L. Mobley

Enjoy Life!

© Darryl L. Mobley

Day 30 Action-Steps

What are your struggles?

_____

_____

_____

What are the 3 Key Ideas that you have after reading this day's tips & strategies?

_____

_____

_____

What 2-3 Actions will you take as a result of your Key Ideas (above) and when will you take those actions?

_____

_____

_____

How will you benefit from taking those actions?

_____

_____

_____

WRITE A LETTER TO THE 'OLD' YOU ABOUT THE 'NEW' YOU THAT YOU'VE BECOME

_____
_____
_____
_____
_____
_____
_____
_____
_____
_____
_____
_____
_____
_____
_____
_____
_____
_____
_____
_____
_____
_____
_____
_____
_____

CONTINUE ON NEXT PAGE

Please complete this and the next page after completion of this book.

Today's Date: _____

What's Important To You?

	How Important to You? *Scale of 0, 1, or 2*	Notes/Thoughts?
Family		
Favorite TV Shows		
Friends		
Fun		
Health		
Higher Power		
Key Relationships		
Parenting		
Personal Growth		
Social Media		
Work/Career		

*Scale: 0 = Not important to me / 1 = Somewhat important to me / 2 = Very important to me

Today's Date: _____

Which Way Are You Headed?

	How Many Significant Actions Have You Taken In This Area In Past 2 Weeks? Scale of 0-1, 2-4, or 5+	Your Most Significant Action In This Area in Past 2 Weeks?
Family		
Favorite TV Shows		
Friends		
Fun		
Health		
Higher Power		
Key Relationships		
Parenting		
Personal Growth		
Social Media		
Work/Career		

Every Day Is An Opportunity For A New Beginning.

Today Is Your Day.

AFTERWORD

We've covered quite a bit through the pages of **Rescue Your Life: 30 Days Between You And A Brand New You!** You will achieve the biggest benefit only when you implement what you have learned. Make these lessons your habits.

Read and reread this book, marking it up with notes about how you will use the insights. Often you will have the biggest idea or personal revelation, during your second or third reading of this book.

If you know that you'll need to enroll a mate or friend in the life changing process, give them their own copy of **Rescue Your Life: 30 Days Between You And A Brand New You!** so that they, too, can mark it up, make notes, and learn.

Finally, please let me know how the "brand new you" is benefiting from implementing the insights you have uncovered in this book. Send your stories, advancements, insights, and questions to me at: Hello@CoachMobley.com .

Enjoy Life!

Darryl L. Mobley

ABOUT DARRYL

Darryl L. Mobley is one of the world's leading life & executive coaches. He's helped achievers all over the planet live their best lives and gain professional success without personal failure. He has been cited as **"one of the best life coaches on the planet!"** Darryl is an in-demand speaker, author, and business philosopher with focus on work-life balance, leadership, personal branding, networking, and mentoring. He is known as the "Bulldog of Work-Life Balance."

Darryl is Co-Founder and President of **Beauty Of The Nile** (go to BeautyOfTheNile.com), the world's 1st skin care line 100% designed for the unique needs of skin-of-color. He is a graduate of West Point, has parachuted hundreds of times, Run with the Bulls in Pamplona, Spain, partied at Carnival in Rio, dived for pearls in Tahiti, competed (by carrying his wife) in the World Wife Carrying Championships in Finland, backpacked Asia, wrestled an alligator, and traveled the world.

As a father, his non-negotiable focus is to be an active, strategic presence in the lives of his children.

Darryl has a **message of success for you**, as well as an empowering style that will take you to new levels of performance, both personally and professionally! Darryl delights in delivering his presentations on **"living a life fantastic."**

Darryl has studied **what makes super achievers and super-achieving organizations different.** He knows what they did to succeed, why they did what they did, their specific steps and missteps -- and he brings these powerful insights to you and your organization in a way that is actionable.

For more information on Darryl, please go to
www.CoachMobley.com

What Can Darryl Do For Your Organization?

As founder of several companies and a leading family magazine, he provides powerful insights on work-life balance, leadership, parenting, family, and relationships.

As a successful host of popular radio & TV shows, his messages have appeal to women and men of all backgrounds, cultures, economic levels, and regions of the world.

Darryl **accelerates the leadership & performance** of organizations and individuals, and helps develop action steps that allow people and organizations to create amazing results.

He's the author of several books and success programs, and creator of the **How To Create A Life Worth Living**™ system, and the **Do Your Brand**™ program for those high achievers who want to create or strengthen their personal brand and achieve more success, income, and happiness – personally and professionally.

As an in-demand professional speaker, workshop leader and expert on peak performance strategies, Darryl delivers success principles to individuals, organizations, and audiences around the world. Industries from advertising, athletics, healthcare, fortune 500 companies, manufacturing, real estate, technology, education and many more have been enhanced by Darryl's messages.

Darryl's philosophy: "Enjoy Life!"

Want private coaching from Darryl? Please email Hello@CoachMobley.com

To contact us about having Darryl present to your organization, please email Hello@CoachMobley.com

CONTACT DARRYL L. MOBLEY

for

- **Speaking Engagements or Training**

- **Life & Success Coaching**

- **Executive Coaching**

- **Life Coaching for Teenagers**

at

Hello@CoachMobley.com

= = = = = = = = = = = = = = = = = = =
ATTENTION: ORGANIZATIONS

Darryl L. Mobley's books, programs, and other products are available at special quantity discounts for bulk purchases for sales promotions, premiums, or fund-raising. For information, please write or email:

Mobley Unlimited
RESCUE YOUR LIFE
8924 E Pinnacle Peak Rd, #G5-420, Scottsdale, AZ 85255
Hello@CoachMobley.com